Chinese Wine

This illustrated introduction to Chinese wine explores the history of wine production in China, the legends and customs that surround it, and its place in China today. Traditionally, Chinese wine and spirits were made from grain, and had three important uses: to perform rituals, to dispel one's worries, and to heal. Today, wine is still believed to have a therapeutic benefit, but the Chinese beverage industry has expanded on a large scale and now includes famous brands of beer and, increasingly, vineyards producing red and white wine for global consumption. *Chinese Wine* is indispensable reading for wine-lovers and all those with an interest in the transition from traditional to modern Chinese culture.

Introductions to Chinese Culture

The thirty volumes in the Introductions to Chinese Culture series provide accessible overviews of particular aspects of Chinese culture written by a noted expert in the field concerned. The topics covered range from architecture to archaeology, from mythology and music to martial arts. Each volume is lavishly illustrated in full color and will appeal to students requiring an introductory survey of the subject, as well as to more general readers.

Li zhengping

CHINESE WINE

CAMBRIDGE
UNIVERSITY PRESS

CAMBRIDGE UNIVERSITY PRESS
Cambridge, New York, Melbourne, Madrid, Cape Town, Singapore,
São Paulo, Delhi, Dubai, Tokyo, Mexico City

Cambridge University Press
The Edinburgh Building, Cambridge CB2 8RU, UK

Published in the United States of America by Cambridge University Press,
New York

www.cambridge.org
Information on this title: www.cambridge.org/9780521186506

Originally published by China Intercontinental Press as
Chinese Wine (9787508516714) in 2010

© China Intercontinental Press 2010

This updated edition is published by Cambridge University Press
with the permission of China Intercontinental Press under
the China Book International programme ⟨logo⟩.
For more information on the China Book International programme, please visit
http://www.cbi.gov.cn/wisework/content/10005.html

Cambridge University Press retains copyright in its own contributions
to this updated edition

© Cambridge University Press 2011

First published 2011

A catalogue record for this publication is available from the British Library

ISBN 978-0-521-18650-6 Paperback

Contents

Preface

The Chinese do not see wine as one of the necessities of life, but the culture of wine has made, and continues to make, an impact on the way the Chinese live. Chinese alcoholic drinks are made chiefly from grain. Throughout China's long history, with its large population and long-term reliance on agriculture, fluctuations in the wine trade have been closely related to political, economic and social conditions. Indeed, successive ruling dynasties either issued or relaxed restrictions on wine production according to the quality of grain harvests in order to make sure that people had enough to eat. In some areas the flourishing of the wine business was not just the outcome of general prosperity in good years, but also encouraged and invigorated the social life of the region. Traditionally, wine had three important uses: to perform rituals, to dispel one's worries and to heal.

Chinese wine making can be traced back as far as c. 4000 BC, to the early period of the Neolithic Yangshao Culture. During its long development, Chinese wine has developed distinctive characteristics. Chinese wine is traditionally based on grains, with only a few wines being made from fruit, while in recent years beer has been introduced to China. Currently the annual beer production of China ranks second in the world. In

Yangshao Culture
The Yangshao Culture was an important Neolithic culture on the middle reaches of the Yellow River. The Yangshao village site after which it is named is in Mianchi County, Sanmenxia City in Henan Province, and was discovered in 1921. The culture existed from about 5000–3000 BC.

China alcoholic beverages are divided into three main categories: fermented alcoholic beverages, distilled spirits and integrated alcoholic beverages. The fermented beverages are divided into the five subcategories of beer, grape wines, fruit wines, Chinese rice wine and miscellaneous others. Distilled spirits include Chinese spirits and spirits such as brandy and whisky.

Archaeological evidence suggests that the period between the early Yangshao culture and the beginning of the Xia Dynasty (2070–1600 BC) were the formative years of Chinese wine making. Inspired by the natural fermentation of fruit, people began to steep fermented grain to make alcoholic beverages, gradually standardizing the fermentation method. From the Xia to the Zhou Dynasty (1046–256 BC) wine-making techniques in China advanced by leaps and bounds, and government officials set up a special bureau to manage wine production.

There are no written records of early wine making available for our scrutiny. But in 1979 in Shandong Province, archaeologists excavated a grave of the Dawenkou culture and found a set of wine-making vessels from 5,000 years ago, including vessels for

Jiaxing Ancient Town in Zhejiang (Fangxin/CFP)

boiling the ingredients, for fermentation, and for straining and storing the product. There were also several different kinds of cups for consumption of wine, suggesting that wine-making techniques at that time were already fairly advanced.

With the steady development of wine-making techniques, the consumption of wine slowly became more popular. This is confirmed by the large number of bronze wine vessels which have been unearthed. During the Shang Dynasty (1600–1046 BC), reveling and carousing were fashionable among the aristocracy. According to a record dating from this time, the *Basic Annals of Yin*, in the last years of the dynasty the ruler, King Zhou, who was much given to drinking and sensual pleasures, had a pool of wine made in which naked men and women were encouraged to chase each other. It is thought that this decadence, and heavy all-night drinking, may have contributed to the fall of the dynasty. Learning a lesson from this fall, the first ruler of the Western Zhou (1046–771 BC) promulgated an abstinence order in the Wei Kingdom, the place of origin of the Shang, thus issuing the first anti-wine regulation in Chinese history. At the same time the authorities appointed a set of officers to implement strict control over the production and consumption of wine. Under the Western Zhou wine was divided into three categories. One was wine specially prepared for ritual offerings, which was fermented for a comparatively short time and then used immediately. The second was wine which had been kept to mature. The third was wine which had been strained.

An old Chinese saying states that "the ferment is the backbone of the wine." Long before the Qin unification of China in 221 BC, the early Chinese invented the technique of using a ferment to make wine, a definite advance in wine-making methods. The ancient classic *The Book of Rites*, which describes the ritual ceremonies of that period, records six important things to watch for when making wine: the grain used must be ripe, the ferment must be added at the right time, while steeping and boiling

everything must be clean, the water must be good, the containers must be ceramic and selected for their quality, and the heating time and temperature must be right. A notable feature of the way in which the culture of wine had developed in the pre-Qin period is the links which often appeared between wine and political and military affairs. Indeed, one saying explicitly connected wine with politics: "The wine of Lu is scanty and Handan is besieged." In the Spring and Autumn Period (770–476 BC), after the state of Chu had claimed hegemony over the south, it's ruler, King Xuan, ordered various feudal rulers to come to his court bearing wine. Duke Gong of Lu was late and did not bring very much wine. King Xuan was extremely angry and berated him publically. Duke Gong did not take kindly to being insulted in this way, replying: "I am the descendant of Duke Zhou and a distinguished servant of the royal house; for me to bring you wine was already demeaning and a violation of ritual, and yet you go on to reproach me and say that the wine I prepared was inadequate. You should know when to stop." He then departed without taking his leave, prompting King Xuan to attack his lands. Consequently, King Hui of Liang, who had long wanted to invade the state of Zhao but had feared that Chu would come to their aid, seized his opportunity and sent a force to besiege the Zhao capital Handan. So it was that when the wine of Lu was scanty the Zhao city of Handan was besieged.

During the Han Dynasty (206–220 AD), progress in agriculture led to an increase in grain production, facilitating a boom in the wine industry. Because of developments in ferment making, different areas used different grains to make ferments, and the range of alcohols available increased. There was inexpensive "ordinary wine," there was "sweet wine" which used a small amount of ferment for a lot of grain and was ready overnight; there was a pale wine called *han*, a red one called *li* or *zaoxia*, and a clear one also called *li* pronounced in a different tone. The people of the Han Dynasty called wine "heaven's bounty," a gift given to men from heaven above. It could delight the palate, encourage

< At the Dragon Boat Festival in 2007, Nanjing residents celebrated the festival in the traditional way by the Xuanwu Lake. Pictured here is the Master of Ceremony sprinkling Xionghuang Liquor to pray for blessings. (Focus/China News)

conviviality and be used to drown one's sorrows. From the Warring States Period to the time of the Han Dynasty many drank with great abandon, enjoying the wonderful uninhibited feelings that wine could produce. In a Han period wall painting discovered in Shandong province, there is a panoramic scene of wine making. A kneeling figure is breaking up ferment with a pestle, one is lighting a fire, one is splitting firewood, one stands next to a steamer stirring rice, while one strains a ferment solution into cooked rice; elsewhere another two have the job of filtering the wine, while another figure uses a ladle to transfer wine into an amphora.

At the end of the Eastern Han period (25–220), the Counselor-in-Chief Cao Cao (155–220) made a gift to Liu Xie, Emperor Xian of the Han, of some "nine-stage spring wine" produced in his birthplace, Bozhou in Anhui. Along with this gift he presented a memorial explaining how the wine was made, which relates that during the fermentation period the ingredients were not put in all at once, but were added in many different stages. First the ferment was immersed, then one dan of rice was added, and then one further dan was added every three days until this had been done nine times. Cao Cao claimed that wine made by this method was particularly rich, mellow and fragrant, and worthy as a tribute to his emperor.

In the following period (220–589), when the Wei Dynasty gave way to the Jin and then a succession of different dynasties ruled north and south, peasants from the north fled south in large numbers to escape disaster, bringing advanced production methods and increasing the labor force in the south. As a result, agriculture in the south of China saw an overall improvement, and economic development provided the basis for rapid improvements in wine making. The transfer of northerners to the south caused the wine cultures of north and south to merge, and a number of famous wines emerged in consequence. Jia Sixie, a famous ancient Chinese agriculturalist who lived under the Northern Wei, wrote a famous treatise on agricultural and other rural technologies,

Essential Techniques for the Peasantry, which has extensive sections on techniques for making wine. He sets out eight ways of making ferment and more than forty methods for making wine, a comprehensive summary of the techniques used since Han times.

Under the Sui (581–618) and the Tang (618–907) Dynasties, wine continued to develop. Sui policies on making wine were fairly relaxed; they no longer limited private production of wine and they abolished the wine monopoly, so that ordinary people could make and sell wine freely. In the earlier period of the Tang Dynasty, Sui policies were continued: no wine monopoly was established, and there was no tax on wine. However, in the middle and late Tang, because the national treasury's coffers were empty, a monopoly on wine was reinstituted to increase the revenues of the central government.

By the time of the Song Dynasty (960–1276) wine-making techniques had come to constitute a complete theoretical system. In particular, production equipment for Chinese rice wine had taken a settled form. From the Southern Song (1127–1276) there is a book called the *Record of Famous Wines* which describes in full a hundred or more famous wines from all over the country. Some of these wines were made in the imperial palace, some in the households of great ministers, some in wine shops, and some in the homes of ordinary people.

In the Yuan (1276–1368), the Ming (1368–1644) and Qing (1644–1911) Dynasties, Chinese wine making reached its peak, and the theory of wine making came close to maturity. The Ming scientist Song Yingxing (1587–1663) in his work *The Exploitation of the Works of Nature* describes how a red ferment is made and includes illustrations of the process, a precious contribution to our knowledge. The ancient Chinese medical encyclopedia, *Compendium of Materia Medica*, makes repeated mention of wine and divides it into three main categories: wine made from grain, distilled spirits and grape wine. The work also collects together a great number of recipes for medicinal wines.

The Qing Dynasty painter Su Liupeng (1791–1862) painted the poet *Li Bai Getting Drunk*, representing the story of how Li Bai (701–762) got drunk in a reception hall of the Tang Imperial Palace but was still able to compose an answer to a letter from a barbarian kingdom.

The Ming Dynasty was a significant period in the history of China's urbanization, when the development of industry and commerce brought a great increase in the urban population. Demand for wine grew steadily, and wine making gradually ceased to be a part of agriculture and became an independent craft industry. During the Ming Dynasty this industry spread all over China, and it is recorded that in Hengyang of Hunan Province alone there were as many as 10,000 small workshops making wine. The existence of this multiplicity of small producers caused the industry to develop as never before, and distilling techniques also matured. The Ming period not only abounded in famous wines, but was also set apart from earlier periods by a notable characteristic: the variety and scale of production of wines for health and healing.

The Qing Dynasty surpassed previous dynasties in the demand for wine and the number of varieties available, and the industry reached new heights, while continuing the eating and drinking habits of the Ming. In a synthesis of China's ancient food preparation techniques compiled under the Qing Dynasty, *The Harmonious Cauldron*, there are more than 100 entries on wine, including a comprehensive description of the techniques for making rice wine. In addition, many miscellaneous sources also record the culture of wine consumption in that period.

In the Ming and Qing Dynasties came developments in ideas about drinking wine. While emphasizing the virtues of wine and moderate drinking, the Chinese were well aware of the great harm that alcohol could do to one's health. In addition, in the late Qing period, China's traditional wine-making arts began to merge with newly introduced techniques for making "foreign wine." The result was the profusion of varieties and flavors that can be found in Chinese white spirits, beers and grape wines today. Yet despite all these advances, China's alcoholic beverage manufacturing industry remained largely a cottage industry, characterized by rudimentary equipment, low productivity, a small operating scale and unstable product quality. Production was largely manual, and there was no laboratory, no large-scale mechanical equipment, and even no electricity or running water. The complex production techniques were passed down by word of mouth, and there were no industrial standards. In 1949, China produced around 100,000 kiloliters of spirits, 25,000 kiloliters of yellow wine, 7,000 kiloliters of beer and less than 200 kiloliters of wine.

Following the founding of the People's Republic of China in 1949, the central government increased its support for the alcoholic beverage industry. As a result, a number of state-owned distilleries, including the Beijing General Distillery Plant, were built; many traditional enterprises and brands were placed under government protection and received investments, and great strides were made in the technology of the alcoholic beverage manufacturing industry. The traditional cottage industry gradually switched to mechanized,

Detail from the Qing Dynasty painting *Evening Banquet with Pupils* by Ding Guanpeng.

The China-France Chateau Vineyard in Shacheng, Hebei features lush vines, fresh air and an enchanting natural landscape.

automated industrial production. After China began economic reforms in 1978, the transformation of the economic system catapulted the nation's alcoholic beverage industry into a period of rapid growth. The industry's operating scale quickly expanded and various large-sized enterprise groups emerged. Since 1993, dozens of enterprises in the alcoholic beverage industry have obtained listings on stock exchanges. In 2008, there were more than 38,000 spirit-makers nationwide, including virtually super-sized distillery conglomerates with an annual production capacity of more than 10,000 kiloliters. There were over 30,000 white spirit brands with a combined total production of 5.6934 million kiloliters, representing an almost 60-fold increase from 1949. In the same year, beer production totaled 41.0309 million kiloliters, representing a 5,800-fold increase from 1949; yellow wine production totaled 809,300 kiloliters, representing a more than 30-fold increase; and red and white wine production totaled 698,300 kiloliters, representing a nearly 3,500-fold increase. Since China's accession to the World

Trade Organization, and because of the influence of Western consumerism, new consumer needs have been emerging in quick succession, and the demand for alcoholic beverages other than spirits has surged. As a result, a fundamental change has taken place in the structure of alcoholic beverage products in China; beer, red and white wine and yellow wine are enjoying a steadily rising market share, and beer has surpassed white spirits to become the highest-selling alcoholic beverage in China. In the new century, China's traditional alcoholic beverage culture has embraced modern trends.

The Invention of
Chinese Wine

Where Does Wine Come From?

It is not easy to trace the origins of the production of fine wine. According to the *Shi Ben* (*The Book of Origins*), an important pre-Qin source, "Yi Di first made wine, of five different flavors, and later Shao Kang made wine out of sorghum." On this basis, people in later times have assumed Yi Di and Shao Kang to be the inventors of Chinese wine-making techniques, and those who make and sell wine have regarded Shao Kang – also known as Du Kang—as the founding father of their trade.

Yi Di's making of wine is described further in three works, the *Lüshi Chunqiu* (*The Annals of Lü Buwei*), a historical work of the third century BC, the *Zhan Guo Ce* (*The Intrigues of the Warring States*), a historical work compiled in the Han period, and the *Shuowen Jiezi*, another Han period work, which explains the origins, composition and meaning of Chinese

Essential Techniques for the Peasantry consists of 92 chapters in 10 volumes. It contains more than 110,000 Chinese characters, including approximately 70,000 characters in the text and more than 40,000 characters in the notes. It also has a preface and a miscellaneous section. The book cites more than 150 historic books and records over 30 farming proverbs. It describes planting methods for crops, vegetable and fruit trees; production of commercial timbers; utilization of wild plants; methods for raising livestock, poultry, fish and silkworms, and methods for their disease control; the processing of agricultural, sideline and livestock products; brewery and food processing; and the production of stationery and daily necessities.

It is a common practice to warm yellow wine and liquor before consumption as it is believed that the heat can help dissipate the alcohol and benefit the human body. (Imagine China)

characters. The story goes that it was the women at the court of the Xia Dynasty ruler Yu who induced Yi Di to make wine. With a great many efforts Yi Di produced a good wine with a pleasing flavor, and presented it to Yu. Yu tasted it and pronounced it not bad, but because he was worried that later rulers would lose their kingdoms if they were tempted to drink too much pleasant wine like this he treated Yi Di with distain and would not allow himself to have anything to do with wine. His concern was that large-scale wine making would result in shortages in the grain supply, which would then affect the stability of the government. Yu was right to be concerned: in later generations there were cases of rulers who forfeited their power partly because of their taste for wine.

There are also many traditions about Shao Kang's wine making. One account tells that he was the grandson of King Qi of the Xia Dynasty 4,000 years ago. He was originally called Shao Kang, but later changed his name to Du Kang. His father was murdered while he was a child. When he grew up he assembled a party of senior ministers at court and killed his father's murderer. Then he himself became king, and did much to consolidate the Xia Dynasty, which lasted 400 years. In his youth he had been an official with responsibility for food and drink. He once put some grain in a hollow tree, and after a time he became aware of a strange fragrance emanating from the tree. It was from this that he worked out how to make wine, and so people regarded him as the inventor of wine making. As for why his name changed from Shao Kang to Du Kang, there is no explanation in the sources.

There is a popular saying about Du Kang and his wine: "One bout of Du Kang's fine wine can make you drunk for three years." Wine-makers, because of their reverence for Du Kang, take him to be an immortal, and his name is synonymous with good wine. It is said that during the Jin Dynasty (265–420) one of the "Seven Sages of the Bamboo Grove," Liu Ling, was a great lover of wine and had an enormous capacity for drinking. Because he was dissatisfied with politics he often went off traveling, and wild drinking was

In the watery towns south of the Yangtze River, local people have a long tradition of making and consuming yellow wine. Small boats laden with yellow wine floating on the river is a unique local sight. (Ni Shaokang/CFP)

part of these expeditions. One day south of the city of Luoyang he found himself in front of Du Kang's wine shop. Looking up, he saw two couplets saying: "One cup for the tiger, and he's drunk in the mountains; two cups for the dragon, and he sleeps in the deep." Along with these lines, which ran vertically, there was a horizontal line which added: "If you are not drunk for three years you don't have to pay." When he finished reading these words, Liu Ling thought: "This wine shop keeper thinks a lot of himself. Since you talk so big, sir, I'll drink you dry—every pot and pitcher." He went in, drank one cup and asked for another. Du Kang appeared in front of him and advised him not to drink any more, but Liu Ling was not persuaded. After drinking three cups in succession Liu Ling discovered that he had no money on him, and so he told Du Kang that he would have to go home to get some cash to pay for him. Du Kang said that instead he would go to Liu Ling's house in person three years later to collect the sum owed. Three years passed and Du Kang arrived at Liu Ling's house to find only Liu Ling's wife. When he explained that three years before Liu Ling had come to drink at his wine shop and had left without paying, the wife flew into a rage, and said "Three years ago after drinking in some shop or other my husband came home and died. So it was your wine! If you want your money, I want my husband!" At first Du Kang was surprised, but after he thought for while he said to Liu Ling's wife: "He did drink my wine. But I think he isn't dead, he is just drunk. Let's go and have a look at him, and wake him up." So they went to where Liu Ling was buried, opened his grave and took the lid off his coffin. An astonishing scene met their eyes. Lo and behold, Liu Ling was sitting up in his coffin with his clothes in good order, and his face was flushed as if he had just been drinking and was sleeping it off. They went close to call out to him, and his lips moved a little. He was whispering with a sigh of admiration: "That's great wine! Great wine!"

So perhaps Yi Di and Du Kang were the inventors of wine making. But a large number of people think that the emergence of

wine was the result of natural processes. In the *Huainanzi* (*The Book of the Master of Huainan*), an important work of the Western Han Dynasty, we find the view that "the delights of the pure wine-jar begin with the work of the plough." This makes a close connection between the making of wine and the cultivation of grain. The Jin Dynasty scholar Jiang Tong, in his *Wine Edict*, states still more explicitly that wine was the result of natural fermentation, and he thought that wine making went back to the prehistoric times. The idea that wine occurred naturally is the explanation which appeals most to people today. Grain was stored badly, and so sprouted and produced molds. After grain of this kind was cooked, leftovers that were kept for some time turned into sprouted grain wine. People tasted it and discovered an unusual and attractive flavor, and then deliberate attempts to make wine began.

Wine in Sacrifice

In China the liquid used in the earliest sacrificial offerings was not wine but pure water, because people had not yet learned how to make wine. The ancients thought that pure water was very precious, a suitable gift for the spirits, and even after wine began to be produced the custom persisted of using pure water as an offering in some sacrifices. When used for sacrifice this water was referred to as mysterious wine.

In ancient times, wine used for sacrifice was divided into two broad categories. One was wine made in the normal way. The other involved turmeric root being pounded into a paste that was added to the grain for fermentation and the resulting wine had a natural fragrance. Normal wine was made of grain and fresh water and, because the ingredients were mixed in different proportions and the maturing time varied, the wines produced differed in color and strength. The ancients generally divided these wines into five categories by color and strength of flavor, giving them different names. The weaker and clearer the wine, the more it was valued.

< Tables are set up on the long street in the Zhongshan Ancient Town in Chongqing to offer wine and treats to locals and visitors to usher in the new spring. (Sun Xu/CFP)

For sacrificial rituals there was a whole set of regulations, which not only stipulated what wines were to be used but also prescribed the vessels in which it was to be served.

The culture of the Shang and Zhou times had the ritual system at its heart, and sacrifice was an important part of this system. The inscriptions preserved on bronzes have a great deal of material related to sacrificial ritual, some of which confirms the classical texts, and some of which supplements their omissions. Sacrificial rituals in antiquity fall into two main types: sacrifices to ancestors and military rites. The offerings to ancestors include regular, reoccurring offerings to all ancestors and particular offerings to the more recently deceased. The most important and solemn of the military offerings was the sacrifice of captives.

In antiquity, especially under the Western Zhou, when major sacrifices were carried out the most important element was the "offerings to the impersonator." When sacrifices were carried out, the role of the recipient of the cult, whether ancestor or spirit, was played by a living person. The choice of person for this impersonator role was strictly regulated. For state sacrifices the part was usually taken by a senior minister, whereas the cult activities of ordinary people were mostly directed towards their ancestors, and an impersonator was usually chosen from among the dead man's grandsons. The impersonator's function was very important and, whatever his original status, once the ritual began he represented the ancestor or divinity throughout its progress, and even the ruler of the state had to make obeisance to him and offer him wine and other sacrificial goods. The impersonator had to sit up on the sacrificial altar while the participants knelt before him, as if an ancestor or spirit had come to visit from another world. These offerings to the impersonator had a profound impact on the later development of Chinese drama.

Sacrificial offerings varied in scale, and their importance was generally reflected in the number of times wine was offered.

Ancestral rites ranked highest, and wine was offered nine times; offerings to the spirits of heaven and earth came next, and wine was offered seven times; the spirits of mountains and rivers and other nature spirits received five offerings of wine.

According to ancient sources, in the cult of ancestors under the Zhou 2,500 years ago, wine was used in the following ways: before every sacrifice, specially designated people prepared the wine that would be needed for the rite. Normal wine and fragrant wine were both required, and of the normal wine they prepared specified quantities of the different types. The total for one sacrifice could be more than 150 liters. At the same time the vessels and implements for holding and ladling out the wine had to be prepared as well. The ladles were generally made either wholly or partially of jade.

At the beginning of the sacrifice, after the participants had taken their places, the first step was to sprinkle fragrant wine on the ground to call on the spirits to descend—the ancients thought that the spirits were particularly sensitive to fragrant smells, and after the wine was sprinkled on the ground the fragrance which immediately emanated would make it easy to attract the spirits; then the ruler would take a jade ladle and ladle out fragrant wine from a full vessel, offering it to the impersonator on the altar who was playing the role of the most ancient ancestor. The impersonator would first sprinkle a little of the fragrant wine on the ground, and then take a small sip, putting the remainder down on the altar. Next it was the turn of the ruler's consort to offer wine to the impersonator, who responded with the same sequence of actions as before. Then the ruler and his consort offered wine in the same way to the other impersonators. The purpose of this part of the ritual was to call on the spirits to attend, and after it was over, the participants imagined that the spirits to whom they were sacrificing were now present. Next they sacrificed one or more pigs, oxen or sheep. After that, to the accompaniment of music, the ruler and his consort from either side of the altar would offer wine to the impersonators and invite them to enjoy some morsels of food.

Then they offered wine again, this time a more watery wine, for the impersonators to rinse their mouths—the ancients customarily rinsed their mouths in this way after eating. At this point the senior ministers in succession offered wine to the ruler and his consort. When they had drunk the wine, the ruler and his senior ministers danced for the impersonators in a display of the state's greatness and strength. Then the princes and others offered wine to the impersonators. The impersonators drank with the princes and senior ministers too, and after this was over they retired, bringing their whole performance to an end.

In sacrificial rituals like this wine was not only the catalyst in making contact with the spirits, it also permeated the whole interchange between the world of the spirits and the world of living men.

The Varieties of Alcohol and Their Appreciation

Alcoholic drinks in China fall into the three main categories: fermented beverages, distilled spirits and integrated beverages. Specifically they include beer, Chinese spirits, Chinese wine, fruit wine, tonic wine and cocktails. Of these, Chinese wine and spirits are the ones with the longest history in China.

Chinese Wine and its Most Famous Varieties

Chinese wine is also called rice wine. The main ingredient is rice or another grain. It is made by steaming the grain, then leaving it to make sugars and ferment, before finally filtering it under pressure. The main chemical components of the resulting wine, apart from ethyl and water, are sugars, glycerine, nitrogen compounds, acetic acid, succinic acid, salt, and traces of aldehyde, esters and amino-acids dispersed in protein. The wine is mostly yellow in color, and is clear and transparent, with no sediment. The alcohol content is fairly low, usually between 12–17 %, and the acidity is between 0.3% and 0.5%. The wine has nutritional and medicinal value as well as being good for use in cooking and it continues to be very popular in China.

There are numerous types of Chinese wine on sale today. They can be grouped, according to the ingredients and methods used, into three main categories: Shaoxing wine, millet wine (such as Jimo Old Wine from Shandong Province) and red ferment wine (represented by wines from the south of Zhejiang, from Fujian and from Taiwan). Although there is a profusion of wines of this type, all with their distinct production methods and local flavors, the production area is mainly centered on the middle and lower reaches of the Yangtze River, and the wine produced in Shaoxing in Zhejiang is the most famous.

Shaoxing Yellow Wine

The producers of Shaoxing Yellow Wine use only the best glutinous rice from the year's harvest and water from the Mirror Lake in Shaoxing, and production is limited to the winter months.

Shaoxing yellow wine being transported to other regions by way of water channels. (Photo by Xie Guanghui, provided by image library of Hong Kong China Tourism)

Into the yeast required for fermentation they mix a kind of pungent knotgrass (polygonum flaccidum) and other rare herbs, and the method includes both drenching the grain and spreading it out on a drying floor. It is a semi-sec wine, orange in color and clear, and on the palate it is smooth, mellow and sweet. It is stored in earthenware jars, which are mud-sealed and cellared, where the wine continues to mature. It can be kept for a very long time indeed, and the longer the better. This product is not only excellent for drinking but is also a wonderful cooking ingredient, and it is often used in Chinese medicinal recipes. There are many kinds of Shaoxing Yellow Wine, the most familiar being *jiafan* or "added rice" wine. Currently, Shaoxing Yellow wine is sold in over twenty different countries and regions, and a greater volume of it is exported than of any other kind of Chinese wine.

The process of making Shaoxing yellow wine. (Photo by Xie Guanghui, provided by image library of Hong Kong China Tourism): Steaming rice (1)→Cooling (2)→Adding water (3)→Distillation (4)

An employee of the Huadiao Liquor Distillery paints the bottle with color glaze. (Zhao Wei/China News)

In the regions south of the Yangtze River, "Nüer Hong" (Daughter Red), a yellow wine, has become synonymous with aged fine wine. A genuine "Nüer Hong" is typically stored in the cellar for eighteen years, which produces an intriguing combination of tastes, including sweetness, sourness, bitterness, spiciness and acerbity. (imaginechina)

The origin of *jiafan* wine is given in a popular story. A kindhearted master vintner often saw the children of poor families sneaking into the workshop and eating stolen glutinous rice from the grains which had been spread out to dry. So at the "grain steeping" stage of production he quietly added several extra measures of sticky rice, and after a time the "added rice" custom became established, the wine produced by this method being a cut above previous wines. Later this master vintner simply revealed the "added rice" secret to everybody, bringing an improvement in production. According to how much extra rice is added, this type of wine is divided into "normal added rice," "double added rice" and "special added rice." Because of the extra ingredients the wine is stronger, with a mellow and slightly sweet flavor, and its alcoholic content is 16%–17%. It is the most prized of the Shaoxing wines and is best served slightly warm.

Nü'er hong or "daughter red" derives from *jiafan* wine, and because it is stored in wine jars engraved with flowers it is also called *huadiao* or "flower engraved" wine. The tradition goes that long ago in Shaoxing there was a tailor whose family name was Zhang whose wife was expecting a baby. The tailor, who longed to have a son, buried a jar of *huadiao* wine in his courtyard, planning to have a celebration party with his relatives and friends when his son was born. But, as luck would have it, his wife gave birth to a baby girl and the tailor was so disappointed that he forgot all about the buried wine. In due course his daughter grew up to be a beautiful young lady, and became engaged to Zhang's favorite apprentice. On the wedding day the tailor suddenly remembered the old wine that he had buried in his courtyard eighteen years before, and retrieved it quickly. When the *huadiao* wine was opened its bouquet was overwhelming and its alcoholic effect was sensational. That is how *Nü'er hong* got its name.

Jimo Old Wine

Jimo is a very ancient county on the peninsula which has Qingdao at its tip. Jimo Old Wine was once called *laojiu*, meaning "rich and mellow wine." The sources tell us that in the Warring States Period (403–221 BC) Jimo was a land of plenty, both populous and prosperous. Their mellow wine, being a drink for sacrificial rites as well as for socializing, was produced in large quantities. Jimo Old Wine was praised by many rulers and emperors, and in the Spring and Autumn Period (770-481 BC) Duke Jing of Qi, when in residence at Laoshan, used it as a sacred material in his worship of the world of the immortals. The First Emperor of Qin, Emperor Wu of the Han and Xuanzong of the Tang all drank it in abundance, and so it is known as the jewel of Chinese wines. By the time of the Daoguang reign period of the Qing Dynasty (1821–50), it was readily available in all the commercial harbors of the empire, and was sold in Japan and the countries of Southeast Asia.

Jimo Old Wine is a semi-sweet wine. It is made from millet from the banks of the Moshui River, wheat-based ferment and mineral water from Laoshan, using ancient methods which involve breaking down the millet into a paste by stirring it with a scoop over a moderate heat, then, after saccharinification and fermentation, straining it under pressure. The color of the wine is dark brown with tints of reddish purple. It is crystal clear and transparent, and viscous so that it clings to the side of the cup and does not easily spill. There is a distinctive hint of scorched grain in its bouquet. The alcoholic content is 11.5%, and the acidity is less than 5%. It is considered to be nutritious and beneficial for health. The finest type is known as *Lao Gan Zha*.

Red Ferment Wine

Red ferment involves red mould growing on polished round rice, and is a specialty of the area around Gutian and Pingnan in Fujian province. The wine is made with high quality white glutinous rice, and the red ferment promotes saccharinification and fermentation. The winter solstice is the best time to start making this wine, and after it has fermented for 120 days at a low temperature and then pressed and filtered, blended and pasteurized, it is drawn off into jars where it is matured for one to three years. It is a sweet wine with an alcoholic content of 14.5%–17%.

Longyan Chen'gang wine from Fujian Province has a long history and is the oldest wine of this type. Its production combines all the most highly skilled traditional techniques of Chinese wine making. It is made with high quality glutinous rice, and uses as many as four different ferments. The process involves first mixing herbal ferment, a granular ferment and a white ferment to make a sweet mash, then adding Gutian red ferment, and the technique includes adding rice liquor in two phases. This produces a sweet wine with an alcohol content of 14%–16%, and a sugar content of 22.5%–25%. Normally it should mature for three years before drinking. The wine is clear and translucent and a reddish brown with the luster of amber. It has a fragrant nose and is sweet and mellow in the mouth.

A bird's–eye view of Pingnan County in Fujian Province, a leading producer of the red ferment wine. (Yu Huijun/imaginechina)

Chinese Spirits

Chinese spirits have been made for nearly 1,000 years. Among the grains used are sorghum, corn and barley, among the root crops are sweet potato and cassava, and the sugar-rich ingredients include sugarcane and beet residues and molasses waste. There is also a long list of possible substitute ingredients, such as rice sugar, bran, rice wash, starch residues, and also ingredients from the wild such as acorns, Jerusalem artichokes, birch-leaf pears and Cherokee rose fruit. Different ingredients result in different flavors. On the basis of the different saccharinification and fermentation yeasts and production techniques, Chinese spirits are divided into three groups: great ferment spirits, small ferment spirits, and bran ferment spirits. The bran ferment type is further divided into solid fermentation and liquid fermentation subcategories. Chinese spirits in general have a high alcoholic content, and are transparent and colorless.

China is noted for its production of white spirits, and the production process involves a number of steps:

(1) Material Processing: To make the best use of materials, improve the yield rate and produce a unique character, all

materials used in the production of spirits are subject to processing with a series of special techniques, including selecting the right mixture ratio for materials. In the popular yeast spirit production process, the basic material processing steps include grinding or crushing, moistening, steam boiling, spread cooling, material agitating, and then fermentation in pots or cellars.

(2)   Starter Propagation: Starters are typically made of cereals with starch (such as barley, wheat and bran), beans, sweet potatoes and fruits containing glucose as the raw materials and culture medium. They are crushed and mixed with water before being cultured at certain temperatures. Starters are rich in microbes and culture medium ingredients. The quality of the final white spirit depends on the standard of starter propagation.

(3)   Alcohol Fermentation: Alcohol is the main product of the fermentation process. Apart from alcohol, other substances synthesized by yeast and other microbes, as well as intrinsic elements in saccharine materials, such as aromatic compounds, organic acid and ester, determine the quality and flavor of the final spirit.

(4)   Mashing: Before they can be used to produce spirits, cereals containing starch substances must be mashed into a paste so that they can be turned into powdered sacchariferous agents of dextrin, oligosaccharides and fermentable sugar. Starter and malt are the most commonly used sacchariferous agents.

(5)   Distilling and Extracting: This is the process by which alcohol in the original liquid is condensed and separated by heating. Spirits with high alcohol content are obtained after cooling. During the course of distilling, the flavor elements in the original liquid will be removed, leaving the final distilled spirits with a unique aroma and taste.

(6)   Ageing and Flavoring: The newly distilled spirits have yet to convert into characteristic substances, and the form of the spirits has yet to become full. Storage in a cellar with a special environment for a sufficient period of time is required, so that the fragrance and superior quality of the spirits can be developed and strengthened.

The ninth pure grain solid liquor fermentation workshop of the Shandong Bandaojing Group in Gaoqing, Shandong, has a gross floor area of 48,262.5 square meters and contains 2,916 cellar pools and 42 distilling caldrons. It has been certified as the largest one of its kind in the world, earning a place in the Guinness World Records. (Liang Baohai/China News)

The Gujing Liquor Cultural Expo Garden in Bozhou, Anhui Province, contains the ruins of ancient liquor making facilities, including the 1,400–year–old Wei Well, the 1,000–year–old Underground Song Well, and a cluster of cellar pools dating back to the reign of Emperor Zhengde of the Ming Dynasty (1515). Visitors to the garden can don ancient costumes and try their hands at the ancient liquor-making process. (CFP)

The process of storing and flavoring newly distilled spirits is commonly known as ageing and flavoring.

(7) Compounding: Semi-finished original liquids of different grades are mixed according to a fixed ratio and then regulated and calibrated to give the final spirits a balanced quality and a distinctive character. Because of differences in the variety, quality and mixture ratio of the materials used, the various steps in the production process may not be completely identical, resulting in differences in the quality of the final products. As such, the job of the compounding technicians is to mix and regulate spirits of different quality levels to ensure the uniformity and stability of the overall quality of the spirit.

The secrets of the production of superior spirits are often passed down from masters to disciples via oral instructions and practice. Some superior spirits, such as Maotai and Fen Jiu, involve a particularly complex production process,

The China Wine Industry Association organized China's first wine-tasting contest, attracting 101 contestants from twenty-eight provinces and cities. The competition ran for half a year and tested both theoretical knowledge and practical skills. A number of outstanding wine appraisers were identified from the competition. (CFP)

and their details are so carefully guarded that even the veteran technicians at the distillery know just some of the "secrets" of the production process. During the agitation process of Maotai, for example, some materials must be trampled by bare-footed young women, and, throughout the process, the use of metallic tools is strictly prohibited. However, the production of spirits is not all about process and technique; the right setting is equally important. Chinese spirits are the product of the perfect fusion of technique and nature. From ancient times to today a countless number of famous types of spirits have been produced in the various different regions of China. If we include just those that are on sale today, connoisseurs would be able to list dozens of varieties, such as Maotai, Wuliang Ye liquor, Luzhou Laojiao, Fen Jiu liquor, Shuijingfang liquor, Shuanggou Daqu, Xifeng Jiu liquor, Dong Jiu liquor, Gujing Gongjiu liquor, Jiannan Chun liquor, Jingyang Chun liquor, Gui Jiu liquor.

Maotai

In Guizhou province there is a place called Maotai Township, which is famous throughout the country for producing China's most famous spirit, Maotai. This spirit, which has been produced for over 800 years, is the most popular of the starchy-flavored spirits. Its taste is made up of three elements: it is dominated by starchiness, combined with a hint of mustiness and a mellow sweetness. It is both smooth and rich, with a long aftertaste. The alcoholic content is 52-4%.

There is a beautiful story about the origins of Maotai spirit. Once upon a time there were only a dozen households in Maotai, and the only rich man in the village lived on a hill by the river, while everyone else lived close to the riverside. Although it had long been a general practice for the households in Maotai to make wine, at the time of the story their skills were nothing special, and the wine they made was generally consumed within the family.

One winter, Maotai village suffered the kind of snow storm that occurred only once in a hundred years. An old woman from a distant place, dressed in rags and leaning on a stick, struggled into the village through the snow. She was cold and exhausted, and needed food and shelter. When she knocked on the rich man's door he turned her away, so she went to a poor man's house by the river. The poor householder did not refuse this ragged stranger, but invited her in to warm by the fire, gave her some wine to drink, and let her stay. The old woman was touched by the family's open-hearted kindness, and while the husband and wife were deeply asleep she revealed to them in their dreams a way of making top quality wine. When they awoke the next day they found that the old woman had disappeared. On further investigation they discovered that the snow outside had stopped, that a red sun was slowly rising, and that a new stream of pure water was running through the village. They made wine using the water from the new stream following the recipe that the old woman had revealed to them in their dreams. To their surprise they produced a spirit of matchless fragrance and purity. From then on their spirits became famous, as did Maotai village. However, the rich man's wine became worse and worse even though he used the same water, and his family went to ruin. The villagers concluded that the old woman had been an immortal who had come down to earth, and to commemorate the way in which she had made Maotai famous the symbol of Maotai spirit became "an immortal woman raising a cup."

Guizhou Maotai Co., Ltd., the maker of Maotai Liquor, is now a public-listed company. (Yang Jian/China News)

In 1915 the Chinese government sent Maotai spirit in earthenware bottles as an exhibit to the World Exposition in Panama. The story goes that at first nobody showed any interest, but then a Chinese official came up with an idea to rescue the situation.

A storage facility of the Maotai Distillery. (Feng Lei/China News)

He deliberately smashed a bottle of Maotai on the floor. Soon the smell of the liquor wafted through the whole exhibition hall, and people began to take notice. Maotai spirit won the gold prize at that exhibition, and from then on its reputation spread worldwide. In 1949, on the eve of the foundation of the new republic of China, Maotai was chosen as the wine for the great inaugural banquet. Today, following sixty years of growth, Maotai has an annual production capacity of more than 10,000 tons in more than 70 varieties, dominating the Chinese spirits market. After its listing on the stock exchange in August 2001, Maotai's annual net profits surged by more than twenty percent for five years in a row, earning the nickname of "China's No.1 Stock" among investors.

Wuliang Ye ("Five Grain Liquor")

Five Grain Liquor is produced in the city of Yibin at the confluence of the Min and Jinsha Rivers in the south of Sichuan province. This ancient city was famous 2,000 years ago for its lychee fruit wine. Time brought changes, and the city's wine-making techniques progressed gradually until in the early years of the Ming Dynasty the first forms of Five Grain Liquor began

Sichuan Yibin Wuliangye Group (Zeng Lang/CFP)

to be made. At the beginning of the twentieth century, a local official in Yibin invited local dignitaries to a banquet. At the meal, a fine spirit was served which had been made out of five grains: sorghum, wheat, rice, glutinous rice and corn. At the time this was called "mixed grain spirit." The moment the jar was opened the spirit's fragrance wafted through the room, and when the guests had tasted it they all said it was wonderful. Amidst the general enthusiasm a scholar called Yang Huiquan said admiringly: "In this spirit the essence of five grains is combined to make a liquid like jade. Why don't we change its name to Five Grain Liquor?" The assembled guests agreed, and that is how the spirit got its name.

The people of Yibin take pure water from the middle of the Min River to make this spirit, and there are strict rules about the proportions in which the five grains are to be mixed. The saccharification and fermentation agent is made from pure wheat by a complex method, and it is matured for several years before drinking. Ancient storage vats of more than 300 years old are used for fermentation. After the spirit is distilled, it has to be kept for a certain time, and it is only bottled and put on the market after two tastings and chemical analysis, followed by very careful blending.

In appearance the spirit is clear and transparent. It has a powerful fragrance and flavor with a distinctive aftertaste. The higher its alcohol content, the higher grade it is, and it is famous in China for its distinctive aroma and flavor. Today, as a leader of China's spirit industry, the Wuliangye Group based in Yibin, Sichuan has developed a wide range of differently flavored Wuliang Ye products, including Wuliang Spring, Wuliang Deity and Wuliang Pure Liquor, catering to the needs of consumers in different regions, from different cultural backgrounds, and with different budgets.

Luzhou Laojiao

Luzhou is in the south east of Sichuan Province. This ancient city is crisscrossed by waterways, and the Yangtze River flows through it from east to west. In the Three Kingdoms Period (220–265) it was already making wine, and was renowned for it: "Everywhere in Jiangyang is pervaded with fragrance of wine." In the Yuan Dynasty Luzhou was already making "great ferment" spirits, and by the Ming Dynasty a fairly complete distilling process had already taken shape. According to historical records, even during the Ming Dynasty Luzhou Daqu was sold as far as Yunnan, Guizhou and Shaanxi, and won the approval of a number of celebrities and connoisseurs. There is a legend about the origins of Luzhou Laojiao.

Once upon a time, an old woodcutter from the suburbs of Luzhou went into the hills to cut wood. He saw a big black snake and a small colored snake locked in struggle. The smaller snake had been bitten so badly that its body was a mass of wounds, and it was already close to surrender. The woodcutter felt sorry for it, and moved in to rescue it, and after it had been saved it bowed its head to him and slipped away into the undergrowth. When the woodcutter had finished his work, he set off home, but night fell when he was only half way back, and he lost his way. A cliff appeared in front of him, and from it emerged a ray of light. Plucking up courage he went forward. To his amazement he found that there was a cave at the foot of the cliff with a wide road leading into its depths. He had just decided to go in and

The bottling line of the Jiannanchun Liquor (Wang Bian/China News)

have a look around when two old men came out of the cave and said to him: "You are the benefactor of our heir apparent, and the Dragon King has been waiting for you. Please come in, sir, and do not delay." The woodcutter went into the cave and saw many buildings. In the middle of the central great hall sat an old man with long white whiskers dressed in a long robe. When the old man saw the woodcutter he quickly greeted him and invited him to sit, and from behind the old man an elegant young man emerged and bowed reverently to the woodcutter in a gesture of thanks. The old man pointed at the young man and said to the woodcutter: "This is my son. He broke the rules of the dragon palace and went without permission to the ordinary world, to wander among its mountains and gaze at its scenery. He was unlucky enough to be bitten and wounded by the big black snake, but a benefactor rescued him—otherwise he would not have escaped with his life. You are that benefactor, and I have invited you to my dragon palace to express our heartfelt thanks. In the palace we have every possible kind of jewel and exotic treasure. If any takes your fancy, just ask and it will be yours." At that point the woodcutter realized that the colored snake he had rescued was none other than the dragon's son. He was given a meal in the palace, and when he finished he took his leave to go home. Just before he left the dragon king urged him to choose a treasure. He examined everything carefully but came to the conclusion that none of these precious things would be any use to him, so he declined and said there was no need to thank him in this way. Thereupon the dragon king picked up from the table a bottle of fine spirit and gave it to the woodcutter, saying: "Please take this bottle, won't you? When you are out cutting wood just drink a cup and all your weariness will disappear." The woodcutter accepted this gift and said goodbye. When he was on his way home he was overcome with giddiness, and fell head over heels. He landed at the mouth of a well, and the spirit in the bottle all spilled into the well. When he came to, he was full of regret, and reaching out into the well he scooped up a handful of water to slake his thirst. He found that the taste of the water was much sweeter and more delicious than it had been before. After that the woodcutter often went to this spring to draw water to drink, and each time he drank he felt refreshed and invigorated. Eventually he gave up cutting wood and made a spirit with the water from the spring, a spirit whose fragrance could be smelled for miles around and which excited the admiration of all who drank it. Its reputation spread to every corner of the city of Luzhou.

Luzhou Laojiao is the classic example of a strong flavored *Daqu* spirit. It is colorless and crystal clear, with a strong fragrant bouquet. In the mouth it is mellow and pure, and at the same time cool and refreshing. It has a lingering aftertaste. The vat in which Luzhou Laojiao is still made was built in 1573 and it is the earliest known wine vat in the country. It is also the one which is best preserved and which has the longest history of continuous use. The distillery, by drawing upon its rich historic heritage, has developed a top-end liquor brand—"Guojiao-1573," which features a stronger aroma thanks to extended storage in cellars.

Fen Jiu Liquor

Fen Spirit from Fenyang in Shanxi province has been lauded as a "liquid jewel." It has been made for over 1,500 years and also has a story attached to it.

In the Apricot Blossom Village near Fenyang there was once a young huntsman called Shi Di. One early summer evening, as he was going past a grove of apricots, he caught sight of a frail girl leaning against a tree weeping bitterly. He went to her and asked what was wrong, and she told him that her family had been struck by a disaster and her father and mother had both been killed. She now had no family to turn to, and it was the knowledge that she had nowhere to take refuge that was tormenting her. Shi Di took her back to the village, and in due course they got married and lived very happily together. One year, when the apricot trees in the village were covered with fruit and a bumper crop was just about to be harvested, there was a violent rain storm. The ripe fruit fell

In the ancient Phoenix Town in western Hunan, local people prepare potent spirits using a secret recipe and offer the products in bottle gourds to tourists. (Duan Changzheng/China News)

to the ground, and immediately began to ferment and rot. The villagers were extremely worried. Soon after, when Shi Di returned from hunting, he smelled a peculiar fragrance the moment he entered the village, and continued to smell it all the way home. His wife brought a bowl of spirit out to him, and when he sniffed it carefully he found that the scent he had smelt on the way home was the very same curious fragrance as was given off by this spirit. He took a mouthful and found that its taste was fresh and pure. His wife said: "This spirit was made with the fermenting apricots. Why not ask your fellow villagers to come and have a taste?" Soon they all gathered at his house and tasted the wonderful spirit. After they had asked him to tell them how to make it, all the households in Apricot Blossom village began to make the spirit commercially, and the fame of their product spread far and wide. It was said that the girl Shi Di had come across in the apricot grove came from the heavenly palace. Tired of the chilly dreariness of the heavenly court, she had slipped away and descended to earth to enjoy the

Sichuan is the producer of many famous types of liquor. The Shuijingfang liquor, with a history of more than 600 years, is a renowned brand targeting the high–end consumer market. (imaginechina)

warmth and tenderness of human life. When she saw the villagers' plight, she had put her special powers to good use and produced this delicious spirit.

Fen Jiu Liquor is a classic example of China's clear, flavored distilled spirits. Its production involves a set of special techniques, each of which is deployed with the utmost care. The fermentation process is long and meticulous, with special attention to cleanliness. The outcome is a spirit with a unique sweet, soft, mellow and fresh flavor.

Shuijingfang Liquor

If Maotai is the "forerunner," steeped in culture and history, then Shuijingfang must be the rising star, continuing the legacy of China's 5,000-year-old distillery tradition. In 1998, ruins of

The Jiugui Liquor, a renowned alcoholic drink of Hunan, is stored in the Qiliang Cavern in western Hunan. The enormous cavern measures 56 meters high, 32 meters wide, and 6,230 meters deep, vast enough to hold tens of thousands of people. It is an unrivalled place for storing premium liquor. Pictured here is a performance of the Nuomian Dance in the cavern to celebrate the opening of the Jiugui Liquor. (Zhang Jiagen/China News)

ancient distillery facilities were discovered underground during a renovation at the fermentation workshop of Quanxing Distillery Co., Ltd in Sichuan. The subsequent excavations unearthed a cellar, a drying yard, an oven pit, a distiller foundation, wooden columns and their foundations, as well as a large number of porcelain and pottery fragments and animal bones. They were part of "China's No.1 Liquor Workshop" which was standing on the site six hundred years ago. The unique local geographic and climatic conditions combine to provide a perfect environment for the propagation of the microbes required in liquor production, and have given rise to Shuijingfang's distinctive characteristics. Using modern microbe technology and taking advantage of the secret ancient distillery recipes, precious fungi have been extracted from ancient lees and cultured, resulting in a premium Chinese liquor. Shuijingfang liquors are known by their smooth texture,

Refreshing beer is China's favorite alcoholic beverage in summer.

unique aroma, elegant flavor and a pleasant lingering aftertaste. Shuijingfang exemplifies the way in which premium brands can be created by tapping into a historic legacy.

Beer in China

In October 1900, a group of Russians built China's first beer brewery in Harbin City, Heilongjiang Province and named it the Ulubulevskij Beer Brewery, ushering in the development of China's beer industry. Shortly afterwards, booming cities such as Beijing, Shanghai, Tianjin and Guangzhou started building their own beer breweries, and then in 1903, British and German merchants built a joint-venture beer brewery— Germania-Brauerei—in the coastal city of Qingdao on China's Jiaodong Peninsular. In 1910, the Scandinavia Beer Brewery was

Harbin Beer originated in China's first beer brewery built in 1900. (Fan Jiashan/ China News)

completed in Shanghai; in 1915, the Shuanghesheng Soda and Beer Brewery was built in Beijing; in 1917, the Xingshi Brewery Company was founded in Tianjin; and in 1935, the Wuyang Beer Brewery started production in Guangzhou. However, these breweries had limited production and sales as Chinese consumers had yet to become accustomed to the taste. Within the brewing industry, hops, malted barley and other main materials were generally imported from abroad, brewing equipment was exclusively foreign-made, and the brewing technology was controlled by foreigners. As a result, the brewing industry had a limited scale and grew at a slow pace. Prior to the founding of the People's Republic of China in 1949, all of the thirteen breweries in China were located in the nation's eastern region. From north to south, they were situated in Harbin, Shenyang, Beijing, Qingdao, Shanghai and Guangzhou, with a combined annual production of merely 7,000 kiloliters. As the Chinese economy continues to surge forward, living standards have been rising steadily, translating into a continuous increase of beer consumption in China. Today, beer is one of the most widely consumed beverages in China. As a result, domestic beer brands have been growing rapidly, and a string of sizable mergers, acquisitions and restructuring has taken place in the beer industry. This has resulted in the formation of various large-sized beer conglomerates, such as Tsingtao, Yanjing, China Resources, and Harbin Beer, all of which boast an annual production capacity of more than 1 million tons. Meanwhile, international beer brands have pushed into China's beer market; they produce or

ngtao Beer Street on Dengzhou Road in Qingdao City. The original ngtao Beer Brewery on the side of the street has been converted the Tsingtao Beer Museum and declared a national cultural tage site. (CFP)

The internationally acclaimed Tsingtao Beer. (Liu Junfeng/China News)

market foreign-brand beers in China, or team up with Chinese beer producers to set up joint ventures. Since China joined the WTO, various international beer brands, such as Heineken, Budweiser, Carlsberg and Asahi, have increased their efforts to tap into the Chinese market. Today, China is home to hundreds of breweries, ranking as the world's largest beer producer for the last seven years. In 2008, China produced 41.0309 million kiloliters of beer.

Leading Chinese beer brands include Tsingtao, Yanjing, Snow Beer, Zhujiang, Harbin and Five Star Beer. In addition, there are also some regional beer brands which enjoy tremendous popularity among local consumers.

Tsingtao Beer

Tsingtao Beer is China's premier beer brand. With a history of more than 100 years, Tsingtao Beer has developed a unique brewing process steeped in German traditions and refined by brewing experts over several generations. Tsingtao Beer is brewed with mineral water from the Laoshan Spring, which contributes to its characteristic soft and sweet flavor. Its main ingredients include the highly soluble two-rowed barley malts, fragrant hops and 25% rice. It is produced using the "double decoction mashing method,"

In recent years, it has become increasingly popular for cities host a beer festival in the sweltering summer. Beer festivals are not only holidays for beer lovers, but also favorite venues for locals to relax. Pictured here is the boisterous scene of a beer festival on the Bund in Shanghai. (Jing Wei/China News)

Yanjing Refreshing Beer is very popular in the summer.

and has slightly more hops that most other Chinese beer brands. The fermentation is carried out at low temperatures using the double-pot method to achieve a moderate degree of fermentation. Tsingtao Beer is immensely popular among Chinese and foreign consumers thanks to its classic brewing process and unique post-maturation technique, which allows the beer to feature a fine and pure white head, a slightly yellow color, a soft and sweet flavor, and refreshing taste in the mouth. Since 1954, Tsingtao Beer has been exported to more than forty countries and regions.

Yanjing Beer

The Yanjing Beer Brewery was founded in Beijing in 1980. Following nearly thirty years of vigorous growth, Yanjing Beer has been the best-selling beer in China for eleven years, with an annual production capacity exceeding two million kiloliters. Yanjing Beer is brewed with uncontaminated mineral water from 300 meters below the Yan Shan Mountains, and meticulously selected barley and premium hops. Thanks to its typical high fermentation, Yanjing Beer features a mild bitter flavor and a refreshing taste. At present, there are more than thirty varieties of Yanjing Beer.

Wine made in China

In China, the practice of using grapes to produce wine probably dates back to the Han Dynasty (206–220 BC) or the Three Kingdoms Period in the Central Plains (220 BC–265 AD). In the early years, grape wine was produced in the same way as rice wine and consumption was limited, although in Xinjiang wine made of grape juice was common. According to *The Records of the Grand Historian*, a monumental ancient Chinese history book, in 138 BC, the Han Dynasty envoy Zhang Qian arrived in the western region, seeing "locals make wine in ceramic pots and wealthy people store tens of thousands of kilograms of wine, which could last for scores of years." The Xinjiang people had originally acquired grape plantation and wine brewing technology from the Persians.

Grape wine is easier to produce than rice wine. However, as grapes are seasonal and cannot retain their freshness for long compared to grain, grape wine-making technology was not adopted extensively in ancient China.

The Tang Dynasty (618-907) saw increased interaction between Chinese and foreign cultures. During this particular period of time, wine was a valuable commodity in the Central Plains and there were stores in the capital city of Chang'an offering wine from the western region. Tang poetry also contributed to the rising popularity of wine. The Tang poet Wang Han composed the following *Liangzhou Lines* in the eighth century: "They are about to

Chang Bishi (1841–1916) was born in Dabu County in Guangzhou in 1841. At the age of sixteen, he emigrated to Jakarta, Indonesia, where he worked as a helping hand, then ran a trading firm, extracted tin ore, and eventually became the richest ethnic Chinese merchant. He was both a businessman and a government official, serving in turn as the consul of the Qing imperial court in Penang and Consul–General in Singapore. To reinvigorate China's industry, he built the Yuehan and Guangsan Railways and founded the Changyu Wine Production Company in Yantai, Shandong. In 1898, he raised funds to build two ocean transport companies, with one in Jakarta and the other in Atjeh.

drink / The finest wine from Evening Radiance cups, / When the sudden sounding of the *pipa* urges them forth. / Don't scorn them, / They whom drunken fall upon the battlefield: / In ancient days or now, how many return who go to war?" This oft-cited poem recounts a feast of border defense troops in celebration of their victory in a battle. Halfway through the feast, news of renewed enemy invasion broke, and the soldiers immediately set out again. The *pipa* (Chinese lute) tunes made the poet sentimental: throughout history, how many soldiers manage to come back alive from the frontier?

During the Yuan Dynasty, Mongolian rulers were especially fond of wine. They decreed that wine be used in sacrificial rites at the Royal Ancestral Temple, and ordered the opening of vineyards in Taiyuan of Shanxi and Nanjing of Jiangsu. They even built a wine cellar in the imperial palace.

The *Compendium of Materia Medica* describes two methods for making wine. One simple method was to "use grape juice for fermenting in the same way as the fermentation of glutinous rice, or use dried crushed grapes if no juice is available," while the other method was similar to the making of ardent spirits by "using scores of kilograms of grapes and fermenting them with raw starters in a caldron by steaming and then collecting the lively red dews dripping off with a container." Wine produced using these methods is certainly not wine in the modern sense of the word. A historical record dating to between the third and eighth centuries AD describes a method of "crushing grapes by trampling" in ancient Gaochang. This method is similar to the technique used by some small wine makers in Europe today.

China's wine production industry did not grow much during the Ming (1368-1644) and Qing (1616–1911) Dynasties. The nation's industrialized wine production didn't start until 1892, when a Chinese business tycoon Chang Bishi (1841–1916) founded the Changyu Wine Production Company in Yantai, Shandong. China then introduced more than a hundred varieties of wine and a vast range of wine making equipment from Europe, and recruited foreign wine specialists. Drawing upon the grape-cultivation and wine-making practices of European chateaux, China produced fifteen varieties of brandy, red wine, and white wine.

A statue of Chang Bishi, the founder of Changyu Wine. (Qi Enzhi/China News)

In the late 1950s and early 1960s, following the founding of the People's Republic in 1949, several varieties of grapes for making wine were introduced from Bulgaria, Hungry and the Soviet Union, and cultured intensively in China. Today, grape vineyards and grape production bases can be found throughout the country, and wineries are growing in leaps and bounds. The North China Vine Cultivation Technology Collaboration Conference in 1975 led to a decision to produce wine in Shacheng, Hebei. In light of the international market and the availability of local resources, the top priority was given to the development of dry white wine. In 1978, China produced its first bottle of dry white wine and began exporting. In 1979, China sent its first wine delegation to the International Organization of Vine and Wine (OIV), the first outreach effort of China's wine industry. In 1998, China published a Chinese version of the OIV oenological standards—the *International Code of Oenological Practices*. Although China had yet to join the OIV, nearly two thirds of China's wine

The Changyu Wine Culture Museum showcases brandy and wine produced by Changyu Wine Brewery and offers fine wine to visitors. (Liu Yazhong/CFP)

markers marked "Conforming to the OIV's Code of Oenological Practice" on their product packaging and publicity. In 2001, China's wine production, sales revenues, profits and taxes exceeded those of spirits for the first time. With the rapid expansion of China's wine market, vineyards and wine-making facilities have sprung up across the country from the coast of the Bohai Sea and the Yellow Sea in the east and Xinjiang to the west. High-end products including Grand Cru and Eiswein have also been brought to China. Among the vast array of China wine brands, the most popular are Changyu Cabernet and Great Wall Wine.

A dazzling array of wine

Changyu Cabernet

In 1892, Chang Bishi founded Changyu Wine Production Company with an investment of 3 million tael of silver. The company business license was personally approved and signed by Li Hongzhang (1823–1901), Viceroy of Zhili of the Great Qing Empire, and Wang Wenshao, a high-ranking Qing court official. Weng Tonghe (1830–1904), the tutor of Emperor Guangxu (on the throne from 1875–1908), a high–ranking official with the Ministry of Revenues, and later Minister of Defense, personally inscribed the name of the company. The company name, *Changyu*, consists of *Chang*, the founder's surname, and *Yu*, meaning "prosperity." Changyu Wine Production Company ushered in China's industrialized production of wine. In 1905, Changyu completed what was then Asia's largest underground wine cellar, and in 1914, it officially opened for business. In 1915, Changyu's brandy, rose wine, Traminer and Riesling won four gold medals and excellence certificates at the Panama

A view of the interior of a cellar at the Great Wall Brewery. (Jiguo/CFP)

Catholicism was brought to Yanjing in 1865 and has been practiced here for nearly 150 years. The Yanjing Catholic Church, featuring Tibetan–style carvings, is the only one in Tibet. It is located by the Yunnan–Tibet Highway.

Pacific International Exposition, marking the first international recognition of Chinese wine.

Committed to blending Chinese and Western wine production techniques, Changyu's founder introduced fine varieties of grapes from abroad and transplanted them onto China's mountain grapes, successfully developing a superior variety of grape, "Cabernet Gernischt" in 1931. It remains China's only internationally recognized variety of grape for wine production. Using Cabernet Gernischt as the main material, Changyu produced a red wine with a totally different flavor. To give it a stylish, memorable name, then Changyu manager Xu Wangzhi created a transliteration of cabernet—*Jie Bai Na*, drawing upon the Chinese proverb that "All rivers flow into the sea." In 1937, Changyu obtained government approval to register the Chinese version of the term "cabernet" as its brand. For more than seventy years since then, Changyu has been using the Chinese version of the term "cabernet" as a brand and a registered trademark. Changyu *Jie Bai Na* features a dense aroma reminiscent of pepper and blackcurrant, giving drinkers a "flavor like that of green grass harvested after a rain." It delivers a sour initial taste and a flavorsome mouth-feel that lingers long after the wine has been swallowed.

Today, the Changyu Group is the largest wine producer in China, and indeed in Asia, turning out more than 80,000 kiloliters of wine annually, which enjoy brisk sales throughout China and are distributed to more than twenty countries and regions around the world.

Great Wall Wine

The early 1980s witnessed the takeoff of China's wine industry and the rise of a number of wine makers. In 1983, China Great Wall Wine Co., Ltd. was founded at Shacheng Town in Hebei Province, dubbed "China's Capital of Wine." Great Wall is credited with the production of China's first dry white wine. In 1988, China's first professional dry red wine maker, Huaxia Great Wall Wine Co., Ltd., was founded in Changli County in Hubei Province. At

The wine products of the China Great Wall Wine Co., Ltd. (Zhuiying/China News)

present, Great Wall produces more than fifty varieties of wine, including dry red, dry white and sparkling. Its products are sold throughout China and exported to more than twenty countries and regions around the world, accounting for over forty percent of China's total wine exports.

Yanjing Wine

Yanjing Village in Tibet, 2,700 meters above sea level, is the gateway to Tibet on the "Ancient Tea Horse Road." For centuries, the Nahsis lived here side by side with the Tibetans. During the 1860s, several French missionaries, disguised as merchants, arrived at this land which practiced Tibetan Buddhism and Dongba. They built a Catholic church, which remains the only one in Tibet. They also brought grape seeds and imparted Bordeaux wine-making techniques to local followers. Today, sixty-nine percent of people at Yanjing practice Catholicism and the "Basilica of Our Lady" retains its wine-making tradition, producing about 150 liters per year.

Great Wall Chateau Sun God

Chateau Changyu Afip is located on the sunny slope of a mountain in Miyun, Beijing.

A New Force in the World Wine Landscape

Mr Robert Tinlot, Senior Council Chairman and Honorary President of the Amorim Academy, who personally selected the site for Chateau Changyu AFIP.

At the end of the 1990s, China's wine industry switched its attention from traditional wine to Grand Cru, ushering in a "chateau movement" across the country. During this period, Chateau Changyu AFIP in Miyun, Beijing, whose site had been personally selected by the former OIV President Robert Tinlot, was completed. This was followed by Bodega Langes in Changli, Hebei, the China-France Pilot Farm of Viniculture and Wine-making in Shacheng, Hebei (a collaborative project between Chinese and French governments, also known as the China-France Chateau), the Grace Vineyard in Shanxi; Rongchen Vineyard in Shacheng, Hebei, Chateau Changyu-Castel in Yantai, Shandong and the Great Wall Chateau Sun God, a top-end chateau built by COFCO Wine in Shacheng, Hebei. In 2007, Chateau Changyu AFIP

Chateau Changyu AFIP
Wine

Cabernet Sauvignon is the variety
of grape which has been cultivated
for the longest period of time. It
was introduced to China in 1892
and enjoyed an explosive growth in
the 1990s. Today, it is cultivated in
more than ten Chinese provinces,
including Hebei, Xinjiang, Ningxia,
Shandong, Gansu and Sichuan.

hosted China's first wine-tasting event, showcasing premium wine produced with Cabernet Sauvignon grapes. "The ever-expanding high-end consumer market, the growing premium vineyards, and the flow of international wine-making talent to China, will create favorable conditions to facilitate the rise of Chinese chateaux. In China, world-class chateaux, like Chateau Changyu AFIP in Beijing, are rising rapidly," said Robert Tinlot, Senior Council Chairman and Honorary President of the Amorim Academy, during the fifteenth Vinexpo International Fair in Bordeaux, France.

As the premier chateau in China, Chateau Changyu Afip also offers a "private cellar" service, giving wine storage spaces in its cellars to private patrons. The service features professional wine storage and provides premium AFIP wine. Private patrons can even hold wine parties in the cellar to share their prized wine with their friends. This service has been gaining popularity among the wealthy in China, and is emerging as a new way of socializing.

Wine Drinking Rituals and Customs

The *Jia*, a bronze wine vessel for sacrificial ceremonies, immensely popular during the Shang Dynasty, currently on display at the Anhui Provincial Museum. (imaginechina)

You

A *You* is a container for Chang wine. Chang wine was produced with curcuma roots and black millet, featuring a yellowish color and strong aroma, and was highly prized. *You* were popular in the late Shang Dynasty and early Western Zhou Dynasty, but were phased out from the array of bronze rite vessels in the middle of the Western Zhou Dynasty. *You* were typically equipped with a handle; it had an oval or round shape and might be shaped like a bird or animal. It might also be square, though this was rare.

Since ancient times there have always been numerous ritual rules associated with wine drinking and banquets in China. In ancient society, with its view of wine as an instrument of ritual, the hierarchical code, in which the old took precedence over the young and the lowly deferred to their betters, was observed with special solemnity on such occasions. There were clear rules which took account of the social status and ages of the drinkers and also of the circumstances and season of the party and the type of wine and the drinking vessels. Whether it was a state banquet or a private occasion, there were rules of conduct shaped by the characteristics of the period.

"Flagon Fine and Goblet Rare"

There is an old Chinese saying that states that if you do not have wine vessels you do not have the means to drink wine. Wine vessels were always closely related to ritual vessels, and if the Chinese have always been particular about having fine tableware for fine food, they have been yet more particular about having elegant drinking vessels that were just right for the purpose. For this reason, from antiquity to the present day there has been an enormous variety of drinking vessels of every shape and form, from earthenware to bronze, porcelain and jade, not only embodying the ritual customs of their period but also, in many cases, displaying an artistry that ranks them among the finest products of their age. Drinking vessels came to be an indispensable element of the culture of drinking.

Broadly speaking, the history of Chinese wine vessels can be divided into five periods.

1. The Neolithic period: primitive wine vessels appeared, and early forms of pottery wine vessels emerged.

2. The Xia, Shang and Zhou: the evolution of bronze vessels went through a whole cycle from beginnings through development and maturity to gradual decline. In the early and middle Shang bronze vessels were already used widely as ritual vessels, and at the time of use a certain ordered specialization of function had appeared in the way they were used, showing that the bronze vessel system was taking shape. The late Shang was the golden age of bronze art, and by this period the types and shapes of bronze vessels had reached their classic form and their functions were clearly defined. The relationship between the utensils in line with the requirements of ritual had also been established.

3. The Eastern Zhou, the Qin and the Han: lacquerware was the most common material for wine vessels, and porcelain wine vessels began to be made.

4. The Wei, Jin, and Southern and Northern Dynasties to the Sui and Tang: most wine vessels were made of porcelain, but during the Sui and Tang there was a fashion for gold and silver vessels.

5. The Song, Yuan, Ming and Qing: as porcelain making reached its peak, all kinds of porcelain vessels emerged to take the place of older forms.

In 1979, at a Dawenkou Culture burial site in Shandong Province, archaeologists unearthed a full set of wine vessels 5,000 years old. Among them were wine cups of considerable beauty, some small and bowl-shaped with round handles, some perforated and standing on tall stems. Because wine in the early period was not strained but had a sticky, semi-solid

Jue

A *Jue* is one of the earliest known bronze wine vessels. A Jue was unearthed from the ruins of Erlitou culture in the late Xia Dynasty (from the former site of an ancient civilization at Erlitou Village in Yanshi, Luoyang, Henan, dating back about 3,500 to 3,800 years). *Jue* were most popular during the Shang Dynasty as the most basic of bronze ritual vessels. *Jue* were less frequently used in the Western Zhou Dynasty and were almost phased out by the middle of the Western Zhou Dynasty.

A bronze Jun with a beast-mask pattern, dating to the early Western Zhou Dynasty, currently on display at the Anhui Provincial Museum. (imaginechina)

consistency, often the sources in their references to wine talk of "eating" not "drinking." For this kind of wine, bowl-shaped vessels were more convenient for ladling and drinking. For convenience of shaping, early wine vessels were made of lacquered bamboo as well as of pottery. Pottery vessels were the more numerous of the two, and with the development of the art of pottery making they went through a series of styles, from colored ware to grey ware, to red ware, to white ware, to black ware. The most frequent shapes were the *Hu*, *Zun* and *Gu*, and the black ware period saw the appearance of black pottery cups shaped like egg-shells.

A bronze *Jue* from the Shang Dynasty, currently on display at the Anhui Provincial Museum. (imaginechina)

The period from the beginning of the Shang Dynasty in the twenty-first century BC to the end of the Spring and Autumn Period in 476 BC is thought of as the period of China's slave society. History based on written records starts with the Shang. "The Xia received the mandate of heaven:" the Xia rulers proclaimed that they had received their political authority by the will of "the lord on high" or "heaven." In the Shang period the rulers declared that their ancestors were closely connected with this "lord on high," even by ties of blood, supplying an explanation for why the Shang kings alone enjoyed heaven's mandate. This idea was expressed in the belief that sacrifices to ascertain the will of heaven could be conducted by the Shang ruler alone, after which he would make heaven's will known to his numerous ministers and subjects. When the Zhou replaced the Shang, the theory of rule by divine right established by the Xia gave way to a new theory of the divine basis of the ruler's power: that the ruler "ranks with heaven because of his virtue."

Zun
A **Zun** is a sizable bronze wine vessel; it made its first appearance in the early Shang Dynasty and was in use until the Warring States Period. It is one of the most durable types of bronze rite vessels. It comes in various forms— **Zun** with a large opening, arched **Zun**, and **Zun** with bird and animal depictions.

Bronze Kettles
Bronze kettles first appeared in the middle of the Shang Dynasty, and for more than 1,300 years until the Han Dynasty, they were one of the most common types of wine vessels. They were highly durable and came in a large range of forms: kettles with handles, flat kettles, long-necked and round-belly kettles, square kettles and oval kettles.

An ornate pot with greenish brown glaze, produced by the Changsha Kiln during the Tang Dynasty, currently on display at the Anhui Provincial Museum. (imaginechina)

This opened the way from a theocratic polity to a secular one. Under the Western Zhou it was thought that ritual did not apply to commoners, for it was the relationships of the aristocracy ruling this society that were regulated by ritual rules. The central principle of these ritual rules was that degrees of kinship, rank, age and the distinction between men and women must be observed, and this changed a political life dominated by the state to that of a clan society made up of enormous clans defined by blood relationships. In consequence, a ritual ideology centered on a hierarchy of clan relationships became central to ideas of political legitimacy in ancient China.

During the Xia, Shang and Zhou Dynasties ritual rules gradually developed into a complete system, and wine rituals were an important part of this. As exclusive ritual vessels, and not utensils for daily use, bronze vessels have a very important place in the history of Chinese culture. The shapes of bronze wine vessels, their detailed specialization of function, their level of artistry, their styles of decoration, and the way they combine into a system all give full expression to ritual ideology. Different dynastic periods or different social strata within a dynastic period preferred different shapes in accordance with their ritual needs, and as the specific content of the rituals changed the preferred shapes changed with them. The types and categories of wine vessels were particularly numerous in the Shang period, when bronze-making techniques had improved and the art of bronze making reached its zenith. Among the most important vessels were the *Jue* (爵), *Jue* (角), *Gu, Zhi, Jia, Zun, Hu, You*, square

Yi, Gong, Lei, Fou, Bu, He, Dou and *Shao*, all appearing in diverse forms, each of which flourished for a time. The period also saw the emergence of specialist craftsmen who made wine vessels for a living, and were called *Changshao* ("Long-ladle") and *Weishao* ("Tail-ladle") after the products they made. Even more significant was the fact that rules for the use of wine vessels as ritual vessels gradually became more elaborate, and, under the Shang, wine vessels were used in all great sacrifices and other major activities, so that wine drinking became a habit of the age. Transmitted texts and Western Zhou inscriptions on bronze unite in saying that the Shang Dynasty fell because of its excessive indulgence in wine. Evidently ritual wine vessels played an important part in the social life of Shang Dynasty as a whole.

In the Qin and Han period, lacquer vessels for serving and containing wine began to proliferate in the south of China, and became the main type of vessel. In eleven Qin period graves excavated in Hubei, 114 lacquer handled cups were unearthed, and in the Han period graves at Mawangdui near Changsha in Hunan another ninety of these cups were found. According to the written sources, people of that period dined sitting on mats on the ground. The large vessel containing the supply of wine was placed in the middle between the mats with ladles resting in it, while the handled cups used for drinking were placed on the ground. In the Wei and Jin period the cups used for drinking tended to be more slender and elongated in response to the more upright sitting posture of the drinkers.

The earliest porcelain was made in the Eastern Han period, when porcelain became more and more common both for making wine and for storing and serving it. As production techniques developed and stabilized, fine glazed porcelain wine vessels with beautiful shapes became an important part of the output of porcelain workshops everywhere. During the Tang Dynasty the introduction of tables brought about a big change in the way

A Qing Dynasty bronze pot with a silver-embedded dragon handle (CFP)

A black-glazed patterned decanter from the Tangut ethnic group in the Western Xia Dynasty. (CFP)

people dined, and this had a knock-on effect on banquet manners. Matching sets of smaller and shorter drinking vessels were made in response to the new situation. Under the Song Dynasty it was customary to warm rice wine before drinking it, and the most frequently seen wine vessels were sets consisting of wine pots and wine bowls used in combination. The Ming Dynasty produced numerous wine vessels with blue and white patterns or underglaze red. The Qing was the time for vessels of *doucai* (contrasting color), *famille rose* and other enamel ware. One could say that each age made its own distinguished contribution to the porcelain wine vessel tradition.

Wine Rituals and Wine Morality

A blue and white porcelain pot dating back to the reign of Emperor Qianlong of the Qing Dynasty (1736–1795). (CFP)

From ancient times China has been a land of ritual, and beginning with the Western Zhou the rituals associated with wine became standardized and systematized. Western Zhou wine rituals were later summarized in four words: timeliness, precedence, measure and regulation. "Timeliness" meant that there were proper times for drinking wine—wine could be drunk only at capping ceremonies, weddings, funerals, sacrifices and celebrations. "Precedence" meant that when wine was drunk, an order of precedence must be observed, placing heaven, earth, ghosts and spirits first, and then among men giving precedence to the older and more eminent. "Measure" meant drinking in proper measure, in other words stopping after three large cups. "Regulation" meant that when wine was drunk there was a toast master issuing regulations that drinkers must obey. Infringements of these four principles were seen as serious breaches of etiquette. These ritual rules were based on traditional Confucian moral thinking. Confucians were not against drinking wine. Respectfully offering wine to ancestors and spirits and serving wine to one's superiors and to guests was good moral conduct. But normally people should drink only sparingly, so that food grain could be saved and excess avoided. It could be said that drinking in moderation is the central idea of Chinese wine ritual.

In ancient times when wine was drunk at official banquets the drinking rules were overseen and upheld by the toast master and he could expel

When pouring wine for a guest, it is a gesture of courtesy to fill the cup to the brim. Yet, moderation is the best policy in liquor consumption. It is not uncommon to use larger cups at gatherings of friends to save the trouble of constantly refilling. However, at formal banquets small decorative cups are the norm. (imaginechina)

anyone who broke the rules. In some dynasties, when drinking was conducted under military law, those who disobeyed the toast master's staff were sometimes even beheaded. Obey the ritual rules when drinking and the drinking will be virtuous. When the ancients drank wine they advocated "mildness and self-control." A poem in the *Lesser Odes* of *The Book of Poetry* says "If a man is grave and wise, when he drinks he is mild but self-controlled." Even if he drinks a lot, he must be able to control his behavior and be sure not to disgrace himself by anything he says or does while drinking or after drinking. Similarly, *The Book of Poetry* criticizes those who do not behave properly while drinking, and one poem describes how guests who drink too much become disheveled, come and go erratically, wave their arms and dance, and say things which should not be said. The poem insists that the supervisor of the drinking, the toast master, must keep order to ensure that the occasion remains decorous, and encourages people not to be the kind of drinker who is "senseless after three cups." Another Confucian classic, *The Book of Rites*, records the "three cups" ritual clearly: "When the gentleman drinks wine he takes one cup and his demeanor is solemn and reverent, with the second cup he is gentle and respectful, and when the ritual ends with the third cup he withdraws, cheerful and still respectful, and after withdrawing he sits." At a banquet the chief guest had to observe the "three cups only" rule strictly, and display moderation and civilized courtesy. In the centuries that followed there were changes in the units of measurement and in the strength of wines, but people continued to regard drinking in moderation as an important part of observing propriety and practicing virtue while drinking. In the Qing Dynasty a scholar called Zhang Jinshou wrote a book called *Virtue of Drinking* which was widely read and can be seen as an expression of how people thought about wine at that time: "If people want to drink little, let them; each guest must enjoy himself to the full; strictness and leniency are both advantageous; let each drinker suit himself; do not force people to do what they do not want." He not only referred to the fact that people have different capacities for wine, and that we must respect each other in this, but also said that in toasting and drinking people should not be forced to drink against their will.

Broadly speaking, the ancient ritual of drinking, from palace to commoner, consisted of four steps. When a host and his guests were drinking together they first kowtowed to each other, and when younger people were drinking in the presence of their elders they kowtowed to them before taking their places below them. After the drinkers had expressed their respect for each other in this way, they sprinkled a little wine on the ground to honor the fertility of the earth. Next the guests took a sip of the wine to taste it, and complimented the host on its quality. After that the guests and host alike raised their cups together and emptied them. The custom of making a gesture of respect to heaven and earth when drinking is still observed in some areas with high concentrations of minorities and in some remote villages. It is an expression of man's reverence and gratitude in the face of the natural world.

At banquets there are different terms for different kinds of toast. When the host toasts his guests it is called *chou*; when the guests toast the host in return it is called *zuo*, when guests toast each other it is called *lü chou*, and going round and toasting one's fellow diners in order is called *xing jiu*. The person making the toast and the person receiving it both have to stand up and the toast is expressed briefly in a few words. Generally the toasting stops after three cups. Respect for one's elders while drinking is embodied in the rule that younger people must get the assent of older people before raising their cups; when they are drinking together younger people should not empty their cups while their seniors still have some wine left, and when wine is poured it is done in order of seniority. These customary rules are still observed today when wine is drunk on formal occasions.

In fact, to understand modern wine-drinking manners a good starting point is the way in which wine is poured at banquets. There is a common saying "With wine all the way up, with tea half the way up." This means that when you are entertaining a guest if you are pouring wine you should fill the cup until it all but overflows, and pouring less is a sign of disrespect. On the other hand, if you are pouring tea for a guest it is all right to fill the cup half way up or a little more, and if your hand slips and you fill the cup to the top this can be misunderstood by the guest as a sign that he is not really welcome and you hope that he will hurry up and leave.

When wine is poured, the host or waiter should go first to the guest of honor and then to the other guests, usually circulating anti-clockwise. The pourer stands to the right of each guest and fills them up one after the other, until finally the host himself is served. If a Chinese spirit or beer is being drunk the "fill it up" rule still applies, but grape wine is poured in the customary way. After cups have been filled, before the first cup is drunk it is up to the host to propose a toast. The terms of his toast are determined by the theme or purpose of the banquet, and he can either speak off the cuff or deliver words carefully prepared in advance. If he is at a gathering of old friends, for example, he will speak of the yearning for friends parted and the importance of friendship; if it is a birthday celebration, he will wish the birthday guest health and long years. The words should be brief and elegant, and they should not only express the host's personal feelings but should also be right for the happy, convivial atmosphere.

After this toast the host will generally urge his guests to drink their fill. Over drinks the hospitality of the Chinese is on open display. At business banquets hosts usually press drink on their guests with both politeness and restraint. After the host has proposed a toast he invites the diners to drain their cups; they all stand up and the host finishes the wine in his cup in one go, exposing the bottom of his cup, to show his respect for his guests. After that he invites his guests to drain their cups. This sequence will most often be repeated three times, and is called "the first three cups." With the exception of those who have made it clear in advance that they do not drink, the diners generally have to drink these first three cups in full.

"Returning the toast" is when a guest toasts a host. This is also very important. There is no limit to the number of times it can be done, and this basically depends on the capacity of the guests. If only the host at a banquet proposed toasts and no guests toasted him in return the atmosphere would be very awkward.

"Toasting each other" generally refers to when the other diners toast each other after the host has proposed his toasts and the guest of honor has replied. Etiquette requires that the host should not regard such behavior as a breach of good manners, but he should actually encourage it. Usually at banquets the host hopes that the guests will drink and chatter freely, so that guests and hosts can enjoy themselves to the full.

The Chinese sometimes describe refusing to do something and then being forced to do it anyway as "refusing the toast only to drink the forfeit." This refers to the imposition of a forfeit as a punishment for breaking wine-drinking rules, a practice closely parallel to toasting. These days the most common kind of drinking forfeit is when close friends get together for a drink and a latecomer is forced to drink a forfeit. No real punishment is intended, but the penalty is imposed to liven up the atmosphere.

Because of the stimulating effect alcohol can have on people's mood and conduct, Chinese people have come up with a number of brief codes for drinking. Children are generally not allowed to drink, and when adults drink, the rules most commonly referred to are the "three prohibitions," the "five things to do when drinking" and the "seven things to avoid."

The first of the three prohibitions is on drinking early in the morning, since drinking on an empty stomach irritates the stomach and does harm to health. The second prohibition is on drinking competitions. It is true that the atmosphere can be improved when drinkers challenge each other to drinking games, but drinking with competition as the main purpose is not to be recommended. The third prohibition is on taking part in a succession of drinking sessions in one day or in a short period of time: it is better to drink in moderation.

The "five things to do when drinking" are as follows: 1) When you drink, eat something at the same time; eating a dish with meat is especially good for protecting the stomach. 2) Drink slowly and savor your drink, relishing the flavor; don't gulp it down. 3) Sit comfortably and don't rush around with a glass in your hand. 4) Drink authentic wines and spirits; don't touch anything with dubious origins. 5) Drink in moderation.

The "seven things to avoid" are: 1) Avoid cold drinks. 2) Avoid drinking when you are angry. 3) Avoid mixed drinks. 4) Avoid forcing down drinks that are too strong for you. 5) Avoid baths straight after drinking. 6) Avoid drinking during pregnancy. 7) When fertile avoid sex after drinking.

The Chinese maintain that moral standards apply not just to the drinking of wine but also to the making and selling of wine. Wine makers should carry out the technical processes scrupulously and observe quality standards. There should be no skimping or saving, and everything should be done completely in the proper order. Wine sellers should sell genuine products at fair prices, and should not give short measure. The reason why some of China's famous traditional wines have remained famous for such a long time is that the producers have always put quality first and treasured their reputation. This is wine morality in practice.

Chinese wine has existed for a long time and enthusiasm for alcohol is widespread, but drunkenness is not a serious problem in China. The most important reason for this is that good manners and behavior in wine drinking have been strongly promoted ever since the Zhou Dynasty. When successive dynasties issued restrictions on alcohol, their primary motive was always their wish above all to protect the supply of grain for food, because they did not want the making of wine to threaten the stability of government. In Chinese history large-scale restrictions on alcohol appear fifteen times in the sources, and each time the restrictions were observed, with notably good results. This is a further sign that the Chinese attitude to alcohol is part of a very rational tradition.

Drinking Games

In ancient times the toast master was the official who supervised drinking ceremonies when the royal house was holding a banquet. His Chinese title means "official in charge of drinking orders." Because he had the right to interfere in the way that wine was drunk he was respected by diners. But as time went by it became more and more usual for people to drink for pleasure, and the purely supervisory and disciplinary content of these drinking orders became extended in scope. Scholars and men of refinement played literary games, outdoing each other in cleverness and trumping each other's quotations from the classics. Ordinary people preferred number games, engaging in entertaining battles of wits. So there arose "drinking orders," in which knowledge, intellect, entertainment and instruction were fused. The drinkers following these orders were in reality playing drinking games, amusing and enjoying themselves and increasing the fun of the drinking. In China today, both in the cities and in the countryside, drinking often involves these games, and knowledge of more than one kind is required. Below we will say something about some of the most popular games.

Guess-fingers In every part of China the most widespread drinking game is guess-fingers. Usually two people compete against each other, and the winner does not have to drink, while the loser does. The competitors together each hold a bunched fist out in front of them and then extend some of their fingers, at the same time shouting out a number between zero and ten. If the number someone calls is the same as the total number of fingers extended by both players combined, he wins. If neither player gets the number right, they play and guess again. There are some further rules. Firstly, you cannot stick out just your little finger, since in China this is a gesture of contempt and disrespect. Secondly, if you extend any fingers you must include either a thumb or a little finger. Thirdly, the number you call must be less than the sum of the fingers you yourself are extending plus five. Anyone who breaks one of these three rules loses the round. There is a special rhyme with a certain rhythm which is recited while playing. Because this game is quite complex the players usually agree before they start to play the best of three or the best of five. If a whole group wants to play, generally two players start, and then there is a succession of singles matches with the loser dropping out each time.

Stone, scissors, cloth The "stone" is the hand bunched into a fist, the "scissors" is the hand with the index and middle fingers extended, and the "cloth" is the hand with all fingers extended and with the palm showing. Because scissors can cut cloth, if one player sticks out the index and middle fingers and the other player shows his palm, the one who makes the "scissors" wins; cloth can wrap stone, and so the player with the open hand beats the player with the bunched fist; scissors cannot cut stone, so the player who makes "stone" beats the player who makes "scissors." If the players make the same choice it is a draw. This game can be played by two or three. The loser has to take a drink, and if there are a lot of draws the players can make a decision on whether or not they should both drink. The amount to be drunk each time is decided before the game starts.

Both in the city and in the countryside some people enjoy drinking games (Hongye/CFP)

Tiger, stick and insect In this game, tiger, chicken, insect and stick are used as symbols of gradations of strength. The tiger eats the chicken, the chicken eats the insect, the insect chews the stick, and the stick beats the tiger. Each of the players usually hold one chopstick and beat time with it, calling out the name of one of the four symbols. If two neighbors on the food chain encounter each other, the weaker has to take a drink. If the two names called are not next to each other, then it is a draw and the players play again. The game is usually played by two to four players, but when more players play the quantity the loser has to drink is always increased.

Sevens This is a counting game which can be played by a large number of players. One person starts with "one" and the other players continue, each person in order saying the next number up. But if the number is a seven or a number with a seven in it or multiple of seven, the person whose turn it is will not be allowed to say the number, but must say "pass" or indicate that he is passing by some gesture like tapping the table. When the players get to forty-nine the round is over, and then they start again from the beginning. In other words, when they are counting they are not only forbidden to say 7, 17, 27, 37 and 47, they are also forbidden to say 14, 21, 28, 35, 42 and 49. Anyone who says a forbidden number has to take a drink. This apparently simple game is a tough test of concentration and mental agility. It is rare for anyone to be able to get through a round first time without making a mistake.

The statues game For this game a group of drinkers needs to elect an officer to issue orders. Usually the officer first takes a cup of wine himself; then, he chooses a time when nobody is paying attention and calls out "statues!" At that point everyone at the banquet, whether they are opening their mouths to speak or raising a cup or picking up some food with their chopsticks, must freeze in the position they were in at the moment the order was issued and stay like that for one minute, not making a sound. Anyone who laughs or moves has to drink a forfeit cup. If everybody makes it through the minute, that means the officer himself has chosen the wrong moment to issue his order, and he has to drink a forfeit cup, and then hand over to another officer before the game resumes.

Beating the drum and passing the flower For this game you need a flower and a small drum and someone to direct the game. First someone is chosen to beat the drum, which he has to do with his back to the rest of the diners. The game director holds the flower in his hand and shouts "Begin!" and the drummer begins to beat the drum. The director then takes the flower in his left hand and passes it to his right hand behind his back, then gives it to the player next to him, who follows the same sequence of movements. If the drum beats are fast the players have to move quickly, and if the drum beats are slow they have to move slowly. When the drum suddenly stops whoever is holding the flower has to take a drink. When he has drunk the game starts again with him. Everybody always takes turns beating the drum.

Folk Customs and Wine

In China great importance is attached to events such as birth, marriage, retirement and death and they are always marked with ceremonies of celebration and commemoration. These ceremonies usually include a meal with wine.

In some areas in the south of China people celebrate the birth of a child in the following manner. After his wife has given birth, the husband places meat and a pot of wine in a special basket and carries it to the house of his in-laws to report the good news. When the father and mother-in-law see their son-in-law arriving with these two things they know that their daughter has safely delivered her child. If the spout of the wine pot points towards the inside of the basket, this means that the baby is a boy. If it points outwards, that means it is a girl. The parents-in-law will have prepared foodstuffs like chicken, glutinous rice, noodles and Chinese mushrooms for their son-in-law to take back with him. In some regions the mother-in-law pours all the wine out of the wine pot and fills it instead with rice, telling the son-in-law that when he gets back he should use this rice to make congee (rice porridge) for her daughter. In Jinhua of Zhejiang Province the new father takes the wine on a carrying pole and goes to his wife's family to report the good news, and the in-laws share this celebration wine with their neighbors.

Many regions continue the custom of drinking "third day wine." Especially in the south of China, on the third day after the first son is born family and friends are summoned not just to drink celebration wine but after the drinking to plant a tree together, to bestow on the newborn the good fortune of growing strong and sturdy like the tree. In many places another mother is asked to provide a baby's first mouthful of milk, the implication being that the baby will grow successfully in any environment. Before the baby sucks in this first mouthful its lips are touched with a decoction of bitter herbs, to suggest that in life sweetness comes after bitterness. After the baby has drunk its first milk, it is given a drop of soup made from meat fat, rice wine, fish and sugar, and those present chant these words: "Here's meat—eat that; grow nice and fat. Here's cake—eat it all; grow good and tall. Here's wine— cheers! Wealth and long years. Here's fish and here's sugar for you; your life will be sweet and you'll be well-to-do." This is to wish the blessings of peace, health and happiness on the baby.

In the vast majority of places in China it is customary to prepare a feast with wine to celebrate a baby's first full month or first hundred days. This is the most solemn of the celebrations of a child's birth, and the family and friends who are invited prepare congratulatory gifts. There is a tradition, especially at the end of the first month, of giving the baby its first haircut, and the hair which is cut off is disposed of extremely carefully. In some places it is wrapped in red cloth and taken to the temple, which amounts to a prayer for blessings on the child. The barber who cuts the hair may be invited to the first month banquet, and may even receive a red envelope full of money to reward him for his service at a level far above the usual rate.

The poetic line "When drinking with a bosom friend, a thousand cups are still not enough" depicts the use of liquor to consolidate friendships on joyous occasions. (imaginechina)

A wedding banquet is given the special name of "happiness banquet," and being invited to a wedding is also referred to as being asked to "drink the wine of happiness." Many people choose a place where wine is served for their wedding ceremony, and after the couple has completed the proceedings for the official registration of their marriage, family and friends on both sides enjoy a wedding banquet with the bride and bridegroom. Some newly weds prepare a banquet which lasts several days to thank the guests who come to wish them well. We have seen that amongst the wines of Shaoxing there is a special kind called *Nüer Hong* ("Daughter Red"). One tradition relates that it goes back to a time when a wine-maker buried some wine at his daughter's birth and then dug it up again when she got married. Because it has matured over many years *Nüer Hong* is exceptionally mellow, and it symbolizes all the care which has gone into a daughter's upbringing. The choice of this wine to entertain family and friends at a wedding banquet also stands for the confidence that the bride's parents are placing in the bridegroom and the charge that they are laying upon him—they hope that the new couple will love and cherish each other and that their life together will be filled with blessings. In some places the parents of the bride and the parents of the bridegroom are not involved in their children's wedding celebrations at the same time. The bridegroom first goes to the bride's house to collect the bride and there is a short ceremony: he toasts his parents-in-law with tea instead of wine, and, pretending to correct a slip of the tongue, he calls them "father" and "mother." Three days after the wedding the newly married couple return to the bride's original home to express their respect for and thanks to her parents. On this occasion they drink "return to the threshold wine." At the wedding banquet the bride and groom first have to toast the bridegroom's father and mother and the most important guests, and the bride, when reciting her toast, calls her parents-in-law "father" and "mother." The new couple is pressed by the assembled guests to "drink the nuptial wine cup" together, and after that they go round each table of guests, toasting them one by one and receiving the good wishes of their family and friends.

The Lahu people of Yunnan Province have an unusual engagement ritual. When a suitor goes to a girl's house to ask for her hand, he invites a matchmaker to go with him. They take a well-tied bundle of tobacco and a pot containing around three liters of rice wine. When they get there, the prospective bride's parents invite their relations to come round. They listen to the matchmaker's explanation of why they have come and the tobacco and wine are presented. If the girl's parents approve of the match they receive the tobacco ceremoniously with both hands, and then tell their daughter to get out wine bowls. If the daughter also approves she puts a bowl in front of each person present. The matchmaker then shares out the tobacco, and pours wine for everybody, and they sit and talk while they drink. If the girl does not approve, then her family cannot accept the tobacco, and bowls and wine are not distributed.

At a wedding, after the completion of the civil ceremony, the bride and groom drink the nuptial cup, betokening a long life of happiness together. (Xuedan/CFP)

When the Naxi people of Lijiang in Yunnan Province arrange matches for their sons and daughters, they follow something rather like the ancient custom of sealing a marriage alliance with wine. When a boy is five or six years old his parents go to the temple and after burning incense draw divination lots to choose his future bride. When the boy's parents have settled on a particular girl, they commission a matchmaker to take a pot of wine to the girl's family and propose the match. If the girl's parents agree they wait until she is around ten years old and then choose a day for the engagement ceremony. This ceremony is called "celebrating the lesser wine." The boy's family sends gifts of wine, white rice, brown sugar and tea to the girl's family. After the engagement has been formalized either party has the right to pull out. If it is the girl's side that breaks the engagement they have to pay back the gifts in full, but the boy's side just has to notify the girl's side of their change of mind.

In the Miao and Dong Ethnic Autonomous Prefecture in southeastern Guizhou Province, brides observe the custom of drinking "Road Blocking Wine" before entering their bridegrooms' houses. (Zhang Tianlin/imaginechina)

When there is an engagement among the Hezhe ethnic group, the suitor invites his relations, friends and respected elders, and they travel to the girl's house to ask for the match, taking a wine bottle tied in red cloth and a carp. If the proposal is accepted, the following day the suitor has to go on a formal visit to his future father and mother-in-law and toast their health and kowtow to them. He takes his future father-in-law a horse and a marten pelt as gifts, and also contributes a jar of wine and a pig for use in the party which the family will lay on for their kinsfolk when they give their daughter away.

At weddings of the Bai ethnic group, wine plays an unusual part in the proceedings. When the bride and groom go into the bridal chamber, a middle-aged couple turns up with a pot containing wine flavored with chilli powder and offers it to the couple to drink. When they have partaken, the guests at the wedding banquet are invited to taste this chilli wine. Drinking this wine, because of a pun in the Bai language, constitutes a wish that the couple will enjoy an extremely close relationship. When the banquet comes to an end the guests steal a wine cup from the table and hide it, to force the newly weds to beg for it to be returned. At that point all the guests call out in unison: "What do you want it for?" and the couple always reply: "We're going to need it next year—to feed the baby!" The party then breaks up in a gale of happy laughter.

The Chinese like to celebrate their birthdays, but they do not put this feeling on open display, and it is very rare for someone in his prime to lay on a big dinner for his birthday unprompted. As a rule parents take steps to celebrate their children's birthdays, particularly their first and eighteenth birthdays. When a child has its first birthday it is customary to set up the "grabbing" test. A number of objects with symbolic significance are spread out in front of the child, from which the child chooses three. The choice is

26 October, 2009 was the day of the traditional Chinese festival, the Double Ninth. This happened to be the hundredth birthday of Yang Fengqing of Shenyang City, and her family and friends and over one-hundred neighbors assembled to wish the centenarian many happy returns. (Zhang Hao/CFP)

The Manchu ethnic group in Jilin City, Jilin Province observe the custom of offering sacrifices to the Songhua River, on which they make a living by fishing. The site of the sacrificial ceremony is usually surrounded by distinctive Manchu banners, and traditional dances are performed to the accompaniment of drums and music. Two masters of ceremony read a eulogy, light three incense sticks and plant them in a burner, and then guide the audience to bow three times to the river before two jars of fine wine are poured into the water. The ceremony conveys local fishermen's wishes for a bumper catch. (CFP)

taken to indicate what the child's future likes and dislikes will be and how he or she will make a living. After that the parents invite the family and friends who have come to witness this test to eat and drink with them. Generally an eighteenth birthday is seen as a coming of age, and many parents lay on a banquet on the day, inviting family and friends and their son or daughter's teachers, to express their hopes and good wishes as he or she makes the transition into adult society. Some liberated parents may allow their son or daughter to drink a small amount of alcohol to thank the older generation for their help in his or her upbringing. When adults celebrate their birthdays it is usually a small-scale affair. It is enough to get together with immediate relatives and close friends and have a drink and eat a bowl of long-life noodles. On birthdays a saying is often repeated: "The day the child is born is a hard day for the mother." This is a reminder to the child not to forget his or her mother.

However, when a person turns sixty the Chinese believe that their birthday must be celebrated with due ceremony. In ancient Chinese ideas about commemoration, sixty years was a full cycle, and for this reason the sixtieth birthday is accorded special importance and significance. Children always arrange a sixtieth birthday banquet for their parents, and in many places the sixth day of the first month of the lunar year is chosen as the day for the banquet. The host does not usually send out invitations to the guests: it is up to immediate family and close friends, colleagues, old classmates and neighbors to remember the happy event themselves and go to the house with gifts and congratulations, and the host then invites them to the birthday banquet. On the day of celebration there is a congratulation ceremony before the banquet starts. In the banqueting hall, on the wall opposite the door, the character 寿 ("long life") is hung, and those who are celebrating their birthday, often husband and wife together, sit beneath the character receiving the congratulations first of their children and grandchildren and then of other younger people. For these congratulations the most commonly used words are: "May your happiness be as boundless as the Eastern Sea, may your years be as numerous as the southern mountains." After that there is a burst of fire-crackers and the banquet begins. Because in Chinese the word for "long-lasting" (久) has the same sound as the word for "wine" (酒), longevity wine is auspicious and an essential part of these birthday celebrations. It must first be used to toast those celebrating their birthday, and then the guests drink too.

In China a person's sixtieth year is referred to as the time when "the ear is attuned." The idea is that someone of that age, after a life time of experience, can accept the things they hear with an open mind and heart. In cities sixty is the normal retirement age for men, and given the steady rise in average life expectancy in China someone turning sixty can be seen as just the beginning of old age. For this reason people no longer call someone on their sixtieth birthday a "longevity star," but this term of respect is reserved for seventieth, eightieth or ninetieth birthdays.

The Chinese refer to funerals as "white occasions." Wine is no less essential on these occasions than it is at other times, and funerals in different regions have different wine customs. Since ancient times people have regarded wine as good for opening up lines of communication in the natural world. Traditionally, death is seen as a kind of long journey, whose destination is the nether world and from which there is no return. It is because of this idea and the belief that the soul is immortal that in many regions memorial offerings of wine are made to the recently departed—the living use wine to express their grief and respect. On the day of the funeral procession wine is offered to the departed soul as a token of respect and consolation, and after the procession the host toasts those who have taken part in the funeral ceremony. On the seventh day after the funeral, offerings of wine are made to the departed, and then again on the forty-ninth day, the first anniversary and the third anniversary, to show that they are not forgotten.

China is a diverse community made up of fifty-six different ethnic groups. During the course of China's long history these peoples have mixed with and influenced each other, and there has been a gradual assimilation of customs between contiguous groups. This is true of drinking customs too, but many peoples still preserve distinctive drinking traditions.

Drinking Styles

The Qiang ethnic group live in the northwest of Sichuan Province. When there is a festival they bring out a large container of wine and ask everybody to sit round it in a circle. Each person holds a pipe made of bamboo or reed, which they insert into the container, and as they sit there chatting and laughing they can drink wine from the central supply through their pipe. Because the pipes are several feet long and the surrounding circle of drinkers is quite big, it often happens that many of them suck at once and this makes for an extremely animated atmosphere. After drinking for a while people get up and dance in a circle. The Miao ethnic group of Guizhou also have a similar custom.

The Yi ethnic group practice "turnabout drinking." Whatever the place or circumstances, and no matter whether the drinkers know each other well or are strangers, they always sit on the ground, in more than one circle if the numbers are large. Holding the wine cup in both hands, they pass it round and drink in turn. There is a legend about the origins of this custom. Once upon a time three men from three different peoples lived together on a mountain. One was a Han, one was a Tibetan and one was a Yi. They got on very well together and became sworn brothers, the Han man counting as older brother because he was the oldest, the Tibetan being in the middle, and the Yi man being the youngest. Every year when there was a holiday they got together to celebrate. One year the youngest "brother" collected a lot of buckwheat grains from some land which he had been clearing, and

The Qiang ethnic group in Sichuan is in the habit of "sipping wine," using a straw to sip wine while constantly adding water to the wine for thinning purposes. They also swallow the lees. The wine is made with cooked highland barley, resulting in a nutritional alcoholic drink. Drinking in this manner is thought to be beneficial to the human body. ("Yingjiu Erma" Culture Society/ imaginechina)

The "Sipping Liquor" of the Tujia ethnic group in Enshi, Hubei is a type of sweet liquor made with glutinous rice, maize, sorghum, or wheat. It is often stored in a jar for one or more years and is typically mixed with either cold or hot water before being sipped with a thick bamboo pipe. It is often provided at banquets to entertain guests or consumed to relieve fatigue. (Yang Shunpi/China News)

after grinding it he boiled a large quantity and invited his sworn brothers to come and enjoy it with him. They did not finish it, and the remaining gruel, which was left for a few days, began to give off a strong alcoholic smell. But with "After you!" and "No, after you!" nobody would agree to drink this buckwheat wine, and they went on passing it politely to each other all day. In the end a spirit appeared and told them that as long as they worked hard there would be new wine to replace the wine they finished, whereupon the three men at last began to drink the wine as they passed it.

The Zhuang ethnic group has a traditional way of celebrating birthdays that is still practiced today. This is called "drawing from the urn," and in earlier times this was common among the minority peoples living in a stretch of land which bridges Guangdong and Guangxi Provinces. A thick alcoholic gruel is made in a small urn, and then put away until it is needed for the head of the family's birthday feast. When the guests arrive, a mat is spread on the floor, and then out comes the urn to a place in the middle of the party. Next to the urn they put a dish of clean water,

The Miao ethnic group observes the custom of treating visitors with bullhorn wine. (Qin Gang/CFP)

and when the urn is opened they ladle some water into it. Then they take a bamboo pipe and insert it into the urn, and guests and host take it in turns to suck through the pipe and drink, starting with the guests. The pipe has a valve shaped like a small silver fish which can be opened or closed, and if the liquid comes up too fast or too slowly the little fish can be adjusted. As the party continues they go on adding water. At the end of the "drawing from the urn" ceremony the senior woman ladles some water into the urn, then recites a toast, then solemnly passes the pipe to the guests asking them to have a little more wine—but in reality they are just drinking water.

The Buyi ethnic group like rice wine, which they drink from bowls rather than cups. When they drink they sing, in a call and response style, and the content of the songs could not be more wide-ranging. They sing of the beginnings of things, of the sun and moon and the stars, of the history of their people, and of the mountains, rivers and plants. One person sings a verse and another has to reply, and if no reply is forthcoming a forfeit must be drunk.

Hospitality and Drinking

Mongolians drink *koumiss* (fermented mare's milk). They drink from large bowls in a heroic style. It does not matter whether a guest is a good friend or a stranger; they will be looked after warmly and offered this drink. When they drink they first dip the ring finger of the right hand into the *koumiss* and make gestures of respect to heaven (upwards), earth (downwards) and their ancestors (touching their own foreheads). Only after this brief ritual is complete does the host begin to toast the guests. If a Mongolian host brings his wife to a banquet, this means that the entertainment is being done in style. When the guests arrive the oldest person present takes the place of honor, with guests and host being equally eligible. When the host has poured wine for a guest and toasted him, if the guest cannot finish his cup in one go (non-drinkers have to declare themselves in advance) the host will not accept his cup back, and is not satisfied until the guest has drained his drink. When guests from far away are being entertained, the host or one of the younger people sings a toasting song and usually this song is composed especially for the occasion. To get his guests to drink a lot the host may sing a toast with as many as eight to ten verses, and this is seen as acceptable. If the guests resist the toast or do not down their drinks completely, the song will go on until they do.

Tibetans particularly like wine made from upland barley, which is the main grain crop of their region. Anyone entertained in a Tibetan home must observe the "three mouthfuls to one cup" custom. When the guest is given his cup (or bowl), he first takes a mouthful and the host fills the cup up, he takes a second mouthful and the host pours again, and only when he drinks for the third time does he drain his cup. If the guest really does not drink, he can follow the Tibetan custom of dipping his ring finger into the wine and flicking it three times upwards and to the right. This is a gesture of respect to the world and the spirits, to parents and elders, and to siblings and friends. The host will not only refrain from pressing the guest to drink, he will even show that he welcomes this action. Generally after the "three mouthfuls to one cup" ceremony the guests can drink freely as they please. When guests get up to take their leave, etiquette requires them to drain their cups one last time. On festival days the Tibetans always sing and dance to urge people to drink. If the guests can sing, when they are given a cup of wine, they do not drink it until they have sung some lines of thanks. The host goes on dancing and singing to toast his guests, and if a guest does not want to drink any more he

Visitors to Hailar in Inner Mongolia drink the "Off-the-Horse Wine" according to the local hospitality custom. (Li Shengli/China News)

does a mad dance, pretending to be drunk, to show that he thinks the wine is wonderful and that he has already drunk plenty. This provokes loud laughter from the host and the other drinkers, and everyone feels that the occasion has been a wild success.

The Li ethnic group treats visitors from far away as highly honored guests. If the guest is a man, they drink first and eat afterwards; if it is a woman, they eat first and drink afterwards. Drinking is done in three stages. First people toast each other in an exchange of good feeling; next people drink freely; finally host and guests sing to each other as they drink, and the atmosphere becomes more emotional. When the host toasts his guests he first lifts a bowl of wine in both hands and declares the toast to his guests, then he downs the bowl in one, and finally he holds the empty bowl out and shows it to his guests as a demonstration of

In the Kailige ethnic group settlement in the southeast of Guizhou Province, local people also observe the custom of singing "Road Blocking Wine Songs" to visitors. (Peng Nian/imaginechina)

his good faith. Next the guests drink a toast, and when they have emptied their cups they are immediately served with a piece of meat which is put straight into their mouths. The guests cannot refuse this and must accept it graciously.

The Boyi ethnic group use "call and response" drinking songs between host and guests. The hosts sing words of modest self-depreciation, and the guests sing of their gratitude. Each person sings a verse, and in the intervals between verses everyone drinks a mouthful. Anyone who does not sing has to drink three mouthfuls as a forfeit. As the guest approaches the house the host sets out a table at the main gate and puts on it a pot of wine and some bowls. He ladles some wine into a bowl and picks it up with both hands, singing the "Guest-welcoming Song." If the guest can sing he replies in song. After several rounds of this exchange, from which nobody emerges victorious, the guest drinks a mouthful. When they go inside, if the guest cannot sing he takes a drink for each of the host's stanzas, and they do not stop until he has done this seven or eight times. After they have entered the house, the host

Tianyang in Guangxi is believed to be the birthplace of Buluotuo, the forefather of the Zhuang, and the Ganzhuang Mountain is considered a holy mountain for Buluotuo culture. Legend has it that each year from Buluotuo's birthday on the nineteenth day of the second month in the Chinese lunar calendar, to the ninth day of the third month, Zhuang people gathered on the Ganzhuang Mountain to pay tribute and sing songs, eventually resulting in Guangzhou's oldest and largest "singing fair." Pictured here are local folks drinking the Buluotuo wine at a singing fair. (Xia Xiaohong/China News)

asks a girl with a good voice to sing to the guest as she plies him with drink, and if the guest is a singer he sings a duet with the girl. Otherwise, for each verse that the toasting girl sings the guest must take a mouthful of wine.

Wine and Holidays

Chinese holidays are very distinctive, and one of their special characteristics is the close connection between holidays and wine. At the Chinese New Year, for example, "new year wine" is always drunk; at the Dragon Boat Festival it is the turn of realgar wine; on the Double Ninth Festival the drink is chrysanthemum wine. When a festival day comes along, people like to get together with friends to chat happily over a cup of wine. Against a background of cheerful and happy noise, wine can help people to lay aside the

< A girl of the Shui ethnic group holds a plate, ready to present Jiuqian Wine to a guest. (CFP)

anxieties and weariness of day-to-day life and can bring a joyful atmosphere to the holiday.

The Spring Festival, or Chinese New Year, is the most important holiday in the Chinese year. The activities associated with it start on the eighth day of the last lunar month, and continue until the end of the Lantern Festival, on the fifteenth day of the first month of the New Year. All through the New Year celebrations, from the initial preparations and planning to the lanterns and colored streamers hung out by each household on the final day, there are a number of traditional ceremonies in which wine plays an essential part.

The eighth day of the last lunar month is commonly referred to as *Laba* ("the eighth of the last month"), and on this day and the days following the main activity is making all kinds of preparations for the New Year celebrations. On the day itself people have *Laba* congee, in Han Chinese villages, pigs are slaughtered and bean curd is made, while in the city people give their houses a good clean. In town and country alike this period is used to buy all the things needed to celebrate the New Year, one of which is wine. In some places gifts are exchanged inside the family in the period before the New Year, and wine is the most common gift.

The twenty-third day of the last month is commonly referred to as "Little New Year," and it is the day on which sacrifices are made to the Kitchen God. Popular tradition holds that the Kitchen God is a god sent among men by the Jade Emperor to keep watch on each household's good or bad conduct, and he stays in his household for one year. On the evening of Little New Year he has to return to the Jade Emperor's palace and report what the people in that household have been up to for the past year. He returns to the human world on New Year's Eve. The Chinese believe in karma. Usually every family is under the supervision and protection of its Kitchen God, and on the evening of Little New Year the head of each household presides over a sacrifice to the Kitchen God to speed him on his journey; they pray that "on his visit to heaven he

< More and more people take part in folk events on traditional holidays. Pictured here is a master of ceremony in ancient costume officiating a wine-sprinkling sacrificial ceremony during the Dragon Boat Festival at the West Lake Park in Fuzhou, Fujian. (CFP)

Chinese cuisine pays particular attention to the right combination of foods and drinks. Liquor is considered the best alcoholic drink to accompany hot pot in winter, as it is believed to stimulate blood circulation and make the drinker feel warm. (imaginechina)

will make a good report, and on his return to earth he will bring them continued peace." The offerings are usually of four kinds: a special kind of candy, New Year cake, fodder and water. Some people, who might not want the Kitchen God to divulge what has been going on in their family, smear wine on the kitchen door in an attempt to get the Kitchen God drunk and make him incoherent.

The evening of the last day of the last lunar month is New Year's Eve. The meal on this evening is the most sumptuous feast of the year, and even families without much money and those who rarely drink will get out the wine and celebrate. They celebrate the fact that the whole family has got together, and pray that in the coming year each member of the family will have peace, health and fulfillment. The wine drunk at this New Year's Eve meal is called "reunion wine," and the younger members have to propose a toast to their elders in which the old year is bidden farewell. Before the meal starts firecrackers are set off, and then the eating and drinking begin. The old way of seeing the New Year in was to stay up after the meal playing chess or cards to pass the time; but these days people tend to watch the New Year Gala on television, waiting together for midnight to strike.

The last hour of the old year to the first hour of the New Year is the time for bidding farewell to the old and seeing in the new. Bursts of firecrackers welcome the new spring, and then the individual households make ceremonial offerings to the ancestors and to the spirits of the natural world. For this sacrifice offerings are prepared in advance, and wine, wine pots and wine cups have a prominent place among these offerings.

In February 2008 there was heavy snow in the south of China, and many migrant laborers were unable to return home for the Chinese New Year, so they got together to give the new spring a happy welcome. (Xiaohong/CFP)

Very early on the first day of the New Year people swarm out of their houses to call on their family and friends and wish them a happy new year. Older people usually do not go out, but prepare candied fruit to welcome guests at home. The evening meal on that day is generally a family dinner, and people drink together and wish each other well for the new season. The second day is the day on which married daughters take their husbands and children to the home they left when they married, to wish the maternal grandparents a Happy New Year. They usually take some wine as a present. They arrive in the morning, eat and drink with everyone at midday, and leave before it gets dark. The period from the third to the fourteenth day of the New Year is a time for paying visits to family and friends, and at these get-togethers inevitably wine is drunk.

The fifteenth day of the New Year is the Lantern Festival. On this day, apart from eating sweet dumplings, people also drink wine. Some regions continue the practice of sacrificing to the god

Tianguan and praying to him for prosperity. Traditionally this day is the birthday of Tianguan, identified with the sage king Emperor Yao. Meat, fruit and wine are prepared as offerings.

The Qingming Festival is on the fifth day of the fourth lunar month, a time at which, according to the ancients, everything is bursting with growth. After Qingming the temperature rises and the rains come down, and it is the best time for spring ploughing and spring planting. The traditional activities during this festival are making offerings to the ancestors and sweeping their graves, extinguishing the stove and eating cold food, and going outside the city for a visit to the countryside. Three days before the festival people go and put their family graves in good order. They present fresh flowers and make offerings, placing some on the grave and burning others, and they sprinkle wine. These actions express their loving memory of their departed kin.

The Dragon Boat Festival is on the fifth day of the fifth lunar month. On this day people eat *zongzi*, leaf-wrapped parcels of glutinous rice and other ingredients. Each family hangs Artemisia branches and calamus reeds above the front door, and children are given models of birds, animals, flowers and fruit sewn with brightly colored thread to wear at their waists. In some places the children are given red bibs to wear, with a chart of the eight trigrams (symbols from ancient Chinese cosmology) printed on them. The purpose of all these actions is to avert misfortune. Similarly, to drive out evil and counteract poison, some places in former times used to smear and sprinkle realgar on things, drink wine made with realgar, or set fire to it and use it for fumigation. After the Dragon Boat Festival the air tends to be muggy with humid heat and the fever it brings. Mosquitoes and flies, harmful insects and germs breed and proliferate, infectious diseases spread and other illnesses are easily contracted through the mouth or the nose. Wearing fragrant sachets at the waist, hanging up Artemisia or calamus reeds, and using realgar wine as a disinfectant are all traditional precautionary measures to ward off disease and avert plague. In some places it is customary at this time to drink medicinal calamus reed wine to resist epidemics, which some emperors listed among the seasonal wines of their cellars.

The fifteenth day of the eighth lunar month is the Mid-Autumn Festival. For the Chinese this holiday is second only to the New Year in importance. It falls at a time when many fruits are ripe and ready to pick, when the sweet smell of orange osmanthus fills the air, when the ears of the rice plants are golden in the paddy fields, and when a round, full moon lights up the world. In the lead up to the festival family and friends give each other moon cakes. On the evening of the festival families gather together, drink "reunion wine" and enjoy the moon. There is a popular saying: "The blessed can see what the moon sends forth." "What the moon sends forth" is revealed on the night of the Mid-Autumn Festival. Through a cluster of pearly clouds a procession of dragon boats and painted pleasure-boats paddle out from the moon, and the Chinese believe that it is just possible to make out the shape of eight immortals, male and female, dancing gracefully to the sound of gentle music.

The ninth day of the ninth lunar month is the Double Ninth Festival. This is the day on which the Chinese show their respect for the elderly. The festival goes back to Warring States Period, when during the Wei and Jin hegemony the day was already given over to wine-drinking and the enjoyment of chrysanthemum blooms. The Tang Dynasty formally designated the day a holiday and decreed that the bureaucracy should have a day off to wash their hair and celebrate, while among the ordinary people the fashion was to climb to high peaks and enjoy chrysanthemum wine. One story relates that in Eastern Han times there was a man called Fei Changfang who could foresee the future. A man from the same village, Huan Jing, revered him greatly, and usually followed him around to learn from him. One day Fei Changfang warned Huan Jing that "On the ninth day of the ninth month your family is due for a major disaster. If you can get them to sew reticules full of cornel and attach these to their arms, and then climb hills and drink

The Dragon Boat Festival is also the day on which the Miao ethnic group in Dafang, Guizhou pays tribute to their ancestors. Therefore, the festival is considered one of the most important holidays for the Miao group (also known as the "Yaque Miao" or "Xique Miao"). On this particular day, local people dress up, perform the "Reed–Pipe Dance," and drink the native Shuihua wine. (Zhang Jing/China News)

wine, the damage may be prevented." When he heard this Huan Jing immediately did just as his master had instructed, and on the ninth day of the ninth month his whole family climbed to a peak and drank chrysanthemum wine. When the family came down in the evening, they found that their dogs and chickens had all died a sudden death. Later Fei Changfang told Huan Jing that the family had escaped because they had averted evil by climbing high and drinking chrysanthemum wine, while the dogs and poultry had suffered the disaster that was meant for them. This story had quite an influence on later generations, and many people used to believe that climbing high and drinking chrysanthemum wine on this day was a way of preventing disaster. There is a story that the great poet Tao Yuanming, after he had given up his public career and retired into obscurity, had no wine to celebrate the festival one year, and had to content himself with going out to pick some chrysanthemums and then sitting in his courtyard enjoying them instead of a drink. A famous scholar called Wang Hong who had a great respect for Tao Yuanming heard that the poet loved wine and sent him a jar of fine wine. When Tao Yuanming saw the wine he was beside himself with happiness, and immediately opened the jar and drank without stint. After that the idea for a poem began to take shape in his mind, and he wrote his famous poem "Living at Ease on the Double Ninth." From this comes the age-old tradition of "a white clothed man delivering wine," a saying used to denote the fortuitous act of a friend sending a gift of something for which you have longed. Chrysanthemum wine is made especially for this festival. New chrysanthemum flowers and fresh green sprigs are picked on the previous Double Ninth, then mixed in with grain that is about to be fermented, and wine is made from the mixture. When the next Double Ninth comes round the wine is opened and drunk. Chrysanthemum wine is good for keeping elderly people healthy, and inviting older people to drink it on the Double Ninth suggests that you wish them to be healthy for many years to come.

Wine's Therapeutic Value and Regular Usage

The Chinese believe that wine has the quickest, the most direct and the longest lasting effect on the human body. Over the centuries, a significant amount of information has been collected on the nutritional, therapeutic and medicinal effects of wine. Ancient Chinese books on health preservation and medicine all devoted considerable space to wine. The *Book of Poetry*, written between the eighth and eleventh centuries BC, contains lines about the role of wine in promoting longevity; thus, in ancient China, toasting someone was often seen as the same as wishing someone longevity.

It is thought that rice wine serves the medicinal functions of improving blood circulation, stimulating metabolism, nourishing blood, preserving beauty and causing the muscles and joints to relax, thereby building up the body and promoting longevity. Rice wine boiled with a small amount of waxberry, longan,

The Huanggui Thick Wine, a native product of Shaanxi Province, is a sweet wine made with glutinous rice and yeast. It has low alcohol content and contains the aromatic herbal medicine Huanggui. The wine is the favorite tonic drink of local people. (CFP)

lychee, red jujube, ginseng and ginger is the most popular combination, although there are some recipes specially designed for women who have just given birth, the elderly and people who are physically weak. Although white spirits are thought to have therapeutic effects, traditional Chinese medicine generally holds that "moderation is the best policy:" consuming an appropriate amount of white spirits can promote coronary circulation, boost the potency of drugs, stimulate appetite and diminish fatigue. The therapeutic functionality of rice wine and white spirits has given rise to a wide variety of medicated wines, produced by immersing or boiling nourishing Chinese herbal medicines in white spirits or rice wine.

A cocktail made with China's favorite tea and vodka

However, traditional Chinese medical theory holds that heavy drinking will do harm to bones and reduce one's life expectancy, while drinking on an empty stomach will lead to serious diseases. Therefore, traditional Chinese medical theory emphasizes moderate drinking during holidays and on specific occasions that wine is served in the banquet.

The traditional Chinese diet emphasizes the need for a proper balance between plant and animal foods and Chinese people will usually drink white spirits or rice wine during meals. In recent years, Chinese people have come to recognize that grape wine may help to reduce the risks of vascular diseases, and many families now prepare grape wine for consumption after meals.

Legends of Wine

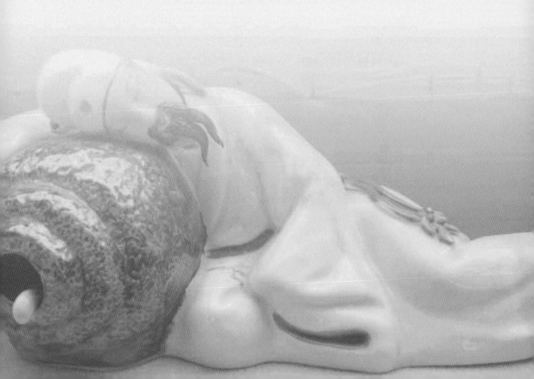

When talking about wine, the Chinese have a variety of different expressions: *bajiu yanhuan* (conversing cheerfully over a glass of wine) to convey their cheerful mood, *duijiu dangge* (lifting my drink and singing a song) to express their passion for life, *jubei yaomingyue* (raising the glass to toast to the bright moon) to convey a feel of being poetic in everyday life, and *zuiwo shachang* (lying in the battlefield drunken) to refer to bravery against imminent danger. The wine in the Chinese legend the *Oath of Brotherhood in the Peach Garden* is a symbol of camaraderie—the wine is drunk to bolster courage. On the other hand, the wine shared with business partners is a facilitator of trust; the wine at wedding feasts conveys wishes for conjugal bliss; the wine shared between reunited friends after a long separation rekindles shared memories; the wine shared with new friends is the catalyst for companionship. Chinese people associate many different experiences with wine.

Wine and Politics

Chinese history is replete with tales about wine. Some people used wine to tighten their grip on power, while some lost their lives and nations because of wine. These tales are thought to depict the personalities, preferences and personal philosophies of many historical figures.

"Pools of Wine and Forests of Meat"

According to the records of later dynasties, the last ruler of the Shang Dynasty, King Zhou, was once an intelligent and ambitious monarch. In his early years, he commanded troops to quell the rebellion of Dongfang Gong and expanded his territory, and his influence spread far and wide. Later, however, he indulged himself in wine and women. He ordered the digging of a large pool on each side of a house where he frequently visited for entertainment. The pool on the left side was stuffed with heaps of lees, twigs were planted in the lees, and meat was hung on the twigs, while the pool on the right was filled with ripe wine. This is the origin of the Chinese expression "Pools of Wine and Forests of Meat," referring to a life of debauchery. King Zhou of Shang was also a ruthless, feared ruler who caused resentment among his people and provoked the uprisings of many tribal leaders, including King Wu of Zhou. His troops crossed the Yellow River in 1066 BC to join forces with other rebellious tribes, and together they crusaded against King Zhou of Shang. A fierce battle ensued on the grassland. However, as some of the generals and soldiers of the Shang Dynasty resented King Zhou they changed sides during the battle and joined the rebels. King Zhou realized that the tide had turned against him and committed suicide by setting himself on fire.

Following the victory, the people of Zhou banned wine in the early years of their rule. According to the ancient history book *Jiugao: Shangshu*, King Wu forbade all officials to indulge in wine, and those engaging in drinking parties could be executed. He also proclaimed to his people that the Heavens invented wine not for people to enjoy, but for sacrificial purposes.

"Sending Wine to Horse Thieves"

One day during the Spring and Autumn Period, Qin Mu Gong (reigned from 361–338 BC), the liberal ruler of one of the five most powerful states during this period, was on an excursion in a horse-drawn carriage. Before long, his entourage found that one of the horses on the right side of the carriage was missing. They immediately set out to look for it. Soon, they discovered a group of natives roasting horse flesh on the south side of a mountain nearby. Upon close inspection, Qin Mu Gong found that it was his missing horse. His entourage wanted to arrest these

> **"The Seven Sages of the Bamboo Groves"**
> "The Seven Sages of the Bamboo Grove" refers to the seven renowned scholars in the Wei and Jin Dynasties named Ruan Ji, Ji Kang, Shan Tao, Liu Ling, Ruan Xian, Xiang Xiu, and Wang Rong. They often got together in a bamboo grove in Shanyang County (the present-day Xiuwu, Henan) for drinking and singing, hence their nickname. All of the seven scholars "abandoned the classics and worshipped Zhuang Zi, and despised rules of rites and pursued freedom." Ji Kang, Ruan Ji and Liu Ling refused to cooperate with the ruling elite, which cost Ji Kang's life.

men, but were stopped by Qin Mu Gong, saying that a ruler should not harm his people for an animal, and that eating horse flesh without drinking wine was harmful to the body. He then instructed his entourage to give some wine to these men. One day during the next year, a battle took place between the troops of the States of Qin and Jin at the same location, and Qin Mu Gong was surrounded by Jin troops. At the critical moment, a group of men arrived and repelled the Jin troops, saving Qin Mu Gong. These men were the thieves that stole Qin Mu Gong's horse the year before. They had come to Qin Mu Gong's rescue and helped him win the battle in an act of gratitude for his mercy on them, and his generosity in giving them the wine.

"Banquet at Hong Gate"

Shi Jhi (*The Book of History*) contains a particularly well known story. At the end of the Qin Dynasty, Liu Bang (256–195 BC) and Xiang Yu (232–202 BC) each led an army to attack Qin troops. Liu's army was smaller than Xiang's but was the first to breach the Qin capital, Xianyang. Xiang Yu was furious and sent troops to attack the Hangu Pass. Rumor circulated that Liu was going to proclaim himself a king in Guanzhong. Xiang Yu grew even more furious, determined to devise a stratagem to crush Liu's troops. When Liu was told by Xiang Yu's uncle, Xiang Bo, about Xiang Yu's fury, he presented an urn of wine to Xiang Bo to wish him health and longevity and flattered Xiang Bo by offering his daughter in marriage to Xiang's son. Xiang Bo promised to persuade Xiang Yu to change his mind and asked Liu Bang to pay respect to Xiang Yu at his camp the following day. The next day, Xiang Yu set up a sumptuous banquet at the Hong Gate. Xiang Yu's advisor, Fan Zeng, was bent on killing Liu Bang and summoned Xiang Yu's general, Xiang Zhuang, giving him instructions to do a sword dance as part of the entertainment and to stab Liu to death during the dance. During the banquet, Xiang Yu grew hesitant and Xiang Bo started a sword dance himself to block Xiang Zhuang from being able to stab Liu. At the critical moment, Liu Bang's chief guard, Fan Kuai, advanced in full armor into the banquet tent, interrupting the sword dance. While offended, Xiang was also impressed by Fan Kuai's bravado, and gave him an urn of wine, which Fan downed in a gulp. Xiang was further impressed, offering him a pork shoulder and asking him if he could drink more. Fan replied that he was not afraid of death, let alone another urn of wine. He then gave a lengthy speech about Liu's accomplishments and how it would be unjust for Xiang to kill him. Xiang Yu was at a loss for words and Liu Bang fled. Later, Liu Bang defeated Xiang Yu, captured the whole country, and established the Han Dynasty. From then on, the expression "the Banquet at Hong Gate" has often been used to refer to a trap disguised as a celebration.

"Talking about Heroes over Cups of Wine with Plums"

The story of "Talking about Heroes over Cups of Wine with Plums" is immensely popular among the Chinese. In the story, the wine was not made with plums; instead, the plums were the fruit to accompany the wine.

In 196 AD, the country was in chaos, dominated by fighting among warlords attempting to gain control of the whole country. Liu Bei (161–223), an emperor's uncle and a relatively weak lord, surrendered himself to Cao Cao, Prime Minister of the State of Han. Cao's consultants urged him to kill Liu to avoid future trouble. Cao knew that Liu was no ordinary player, but feared that if he killed Liu without justification, he would forfeit the public's trust. Cao also intended to win Liu over to his camp, and wanted to test Liu to discover whether he had concealed ambitions. However, Liu was on guard. To avoid attracting unwanted attention, he spent most of his time tending to the vegetables in the back garden, giving people the impression that he did not have any political aspirations at all.

One day, Cao Cao saw that the plums on the trees had turned green and figured that the fermented wine was ready for serving, so he invited Liu Bei to his mansion for a drink. Liu was worried that he might say something improper under the influence of wine

The story of "Banquet at Hong Gate" comes from the *Biography of Xiangyu: The Book of History*, where the author Sima Qian (145-ca.87 BC) describes vividly the open and hidden moves of the struggle that developed between the banqueters as they dined and drank.

and bring himself trouble, so he acted very cautiously. During the drinking, Cao asked Liu who he thought were the contemporary heroes. Liu pretended to have no idea, naming various great men whom Cao didn't consider to be heroes. Cao said that these men were powerful but couldn't be classified as "heroes." He pressed hard on, proclaiming that only he and Liu were the only two true heroes in the world. Liu hadn't expected Cao to see through him, thinking that he might reveal his true ambitions under the influence of the wine. He was so frightened by Cao's remarks that he almost dropped his chopsticks. As luck would have it, thunderbolts were cracking in the dark sky, and Liu conveniently blame his loss of composure on the thunderbolts. Cao figured that a man frightened by thunderbolts could never amount to anything; from then on, he no longer kept a close eye on Liu.

Liu later defeated Cao in the Battle of Chibi. In 221 AD, Liu proclaimed himself an emperor in Chengdu and became a formidable opponent to Cao.

"Removing Military Power by Means of Cups of Wine"

Zhao Kuangyin (927–976), the founding father of the Song Dynasty, was originally the supreme commander of the imperial guards of the Later Zhou Dynasty. In 960 AD, Zhao launched the Mutiny of Chenqiao, toppling the regime of the Later Han Dynasty. His generals draped an imperial yellow robe over his shoulders and proclaimed him the emperor. Zhao drew a lesson from the rise and fall of the past dynasties, concluding that an emperor placing excessive military power with his generals would be inviting mutiny. Thus, he decided to maintain a tight grip on military power to forestall any potential mutiny. Then, one day in 961 AD, he prepared a sumptuous feast to entertain a few senior generals, including Shi Shouxin, who had fought side by side with him and was now a minister of him. While everyone was drinking to their heart's content, Zhao suddenly said to Shi and the other generals, "Without your devotion, I wouldn't be able to be in this position today. Yet, it is very hard to be an emperor; it is far less enjoyable than being a provincial governor. I have a lot of sleepless nights." Shi was startled by his remarks and hastened to ask why. Zhao replied, "It is obvious? Who would not like to be an emperor like me?" Shi rose and kowtowed to Zhao, saying, "We do not understand Your Majesty's remarks. Your becoming the emperor is the mandate of Heaven and all people in our country are loyal to you. Who would think of replacing you?" Zhao explained, "I know you are all loyal to me, but what if your men want to drape the imperial yellow robe over your shoulders so that they can have riches and honors as well. Even if you don't want it, what else can you do?" Shi wept, saying, "We are foolish and cannot think ahead. We beg Your Majesty to point out a path forward for us." Zhao said, "Life is short; it is fleeting and passes very fast. People who seek riches and honors are just attempting to amass a fortune so that they can indulge themselves and that their offspring can lead an affluent life. So, why do you not give up your military power and become a local governor. You can buy fertile land and nice houses in your city, enjoy your life, and leave behind real permanent properties for your offspring. Our sons and daughters can marry each other, and we will no longer be suspicious of one another and live in peace." Shi and the other generals kowtowed to thank the emperor for his enlightenment. The following day, they all tendered their resignation on the grounds of personal health. Zhao granted their registration and made them local governors. Although Shi remained the commander of the imperial guards in name, he no longer had real military power. Thus, Zhao, by offering cups of wine, removed his ministers' military authority without antagonizing them. His move is a famous example of domestic appeasement in Chinese history.

"Lifting My Drink and Singing a Song"

Cao Cao was not only a statesman, but also a great poet. In his poem *Duan Ge Xing*, he wrote, "I lift my drink and sing a song, for who knows if life be short or long; Man's life is but the morning dew; Past days many, future ones few; The melancholy my heart begets comes from cares I cannot forget; Who can unravel these woes of mine? I know but one man... the God of Wine!" The line, "I lift my drink and sing a song," has been quoted frequently to express the desire to make the most out of life. In ancient China, many great men were mavericks who engaged in extreme bouts of drinking and demonstrated their greatness in drunkenness. The ancient book, *Dasheng: Zhuangzi*, claims that "a drunken head speaks a sober mind," arguing that binge drinkers are cool-headed even if they are drunken, and that their unrestrained behaviors and their fondness for drinking set them apart from people who keep to the beaten track and speak and act cautiously, thus enjoying greater popularity.

"A Heavy Drinker from Gaoyang"

Li Yiji, a scholar living at the end of the Qin Dynasty, was highly intelligent and learned but, because of his humble origins and low social status, he struggled to fulfill his ambitions. One day, Liu Bang's rebel forces were passing by Li's hometown, and he thought of joining Liu's forces to accomplish his ambitions. On the eve of his departure, he was told that Liu Bang disliked intellectuals and that if a visitor showed up in a scholar's cap, Liu Bang would grab the cap and toss it into the latrine. Despite the warning, Li Yiji decided to take his chances with Liu Bang and proceeded to Liu's camp. He told the guards at the camp that Gaoying native Li Yiji was requesting to see Liu Bang. Liu denied his request. Li, with a hand on his sword handle, yelled, "I am a heavy drinker from Gaoyang. I am not a scholar." Liu was impressed and granted him an audience. From then on, "a heavy drinker from Gaoyang" has become a synonym for a maverick.

"Ruan Ji Hiding Himself in Wine"

During the Wei and Jin Dynasties, the powerful official Sima and the ruler Cao engaged in a fierce fight for control, plunging society into chaos and people into dire poverty. During this particular period, a group of intellectuals, known as "the Seven Sages of the Bamboo Grove," who specialized in metaphysics and Taoist philosophy, lived in seclusion to stay away from trouble and spent most of their time engaging in conversation and drinking.

The story of Ruan Ji (210–263) hiding himself in wine took place during this period. Ruan, a member of the gentry, was a highly talented poet and writer. He was disgusted by Sima's dictatorship and ruthless slaughter of dissidents, and acted cautiously to avoid trouble. He was forced by Sima to accept an official position, but he spent most of his time reading classics, climbing mountains, viewing lakes and rivers, and drinking, in order to protect himself from political upheaval. Sima was tolerant towards his unconventional behavior and Ruan led a peaceful life. His forced aloofness influenced intellectuals who worked in the government but yearned for freedom, earning him much admiration.

"The Old Tippler's Delight Does Not Reside in Wine"

Ouyang Xiu (1007–1072) was a literary giant of the Northern Song Dynasty and is considered to be among the "Top Eight Prose Masters of the Tang and Song Dynasties." He pushed for reforms in both politics and literature. He was once assigned to an important position by the emperor of the Northern Song Dynasty, but was later deposed for his support for reformists. After he was relegated to the position of chief of Chuzhou Prefecture in Anhui Province, he wrote the famed *Story of Old Tippler's Pavilion*, which contains the following lines: "The prefecture chief comes here and drinks together with his guests; he is always drunk after only drinking a little and his age is the highest of all. So he often calls himself the Old Tippler. The Old Tippler's delight does not reside in wine but in the mountains and waters. He holds the joy of mountains and waters in his heart and finds expression in wine." Frustrated in his ambitions for public services, the self-proclaimed "Old Tippler" delighted in the enchanting landscapes and searched hard for the true meaning of life. The line "the Old Tippler's delight does not reside in wine but in the mountains and waters" reflects the philosophy of traditional Chinese intellectuals who hold that "one should refine his personal virtue when in poverty and help save the world when in affluence."

"Nothing Is More Delightful Than a Glass of Wine in Hand"

This line is from a couplet on a scroll dating back to the Ming Dynasty. The first line of the couplet reads "Nothing is more delightful than a glass of wine in hand," and the second one reads "How many times in a life can one see the bright moon?" The couplet states that the most enjoyable thing in life is fine wine, which is attested by a story dating from the Tang Dynasty. Meng Haoran (689–740), a highly accomplished poet, was offered a job in the office of Prime Minister Zhang Jiuling. Han Chaozong, who was the magistrate of Meng's hometown, also recognized Meng's talents and invited Meng to go with him when he was summoned to the Imperial Court in Beijing, so that he could recommend Meng to the Court. Han even laid the groundwork for Meng by talking about his accomplishments in the Court. However, on the day when Meng was supposed to meet with the officials in the capital, he was drinking with his literary friends. One of them reminded him of his appointment; Meng replied: "I'm drinking and do not care about anything else!" He continued his drinking until everyone was gone. Meng missed the opportunity of a life of affluence because of his fondness for drinking. People considered it a pity, but he never regretted it. His disinterest in fame and wealth, his refusal to ingratiate himself with powerful officials, and his devotion to his friends earned him the respect of great poets including Li Bai (701–762) and Du Fu (712–770).

"The Top Eight Prose–Masters of the Tang and Song Dynasties"
"The Top Eight Prose-Masters of the Tang and Song Dynasties" refers to the eight most accomplished prose writers during the Tang–Song period. They are Han Yu (768–824) and Liu Zongyuan (773–819) of the Tang Dynasty and Ouyang Xiu (1007–1072), Su Xun (1009–1066), Su Shi (1037–1101), Su Zhe (1039–1112), Wang Anshi (1021–1086), and Zeng Gong (1019–1083) of the Song Dynasty. They all produced great works, though their expressive styles were different. They opposed rhythmical prose and pushed for unrestrained prose. Their actions have had far-reaching implications for Chinese literature.

The ruins of the Yang Pass in Dunhuang, Gansu. The Yang Pass was first built during the reign of Emperor Wudi of the Han Dynasty (140–87 BC). It was once a town of strategic importance on the route from the Central Plains to the Western Regions. It appears in *Seeing off Yuan'er on a Mission to Anxi*, an oft–quoted poem by Tang–Dynasty poet Wang Wei (701–761). The poem reads: "A morning rain clears the dust in Wei city; the willows at the inn look fresh and saucy; drink one more cup of wine since west of the Yang Pass, no old friends you'll see." It captures the author's reluctance to bid farewell to his friend. (Fragments of Time/CFP)

Poetry and Wine

Chinese people traditionally viewed poetry as the wine distilled from the mind, and many of the great poems are indeed as aromatic, tempting and exquisite as wine. Since ancient times, poets have produced a large number of poems about wine.

The Book of Odes, China's earliest anthology, contains 305 poems, many of which are about wine. Some of these poems are about drinking to drown sorrows, some are about drinking parties, while others are about sacrificial rites with wine. Wine has long been

Li Sao painted by the contemporary artist Fan Zeng (1938–).

used to convey human emotions, aspirations and philosophies through words. In *The Odes of Chu*, Qu Yuan (339–278 BC), a poet and statesman of the State of Chu in the Warring States Period, wrote: "The world is corrupted, only I am clean; everyone is drunk, yet I am sober." These lines reflect Qu Yuan's noble character and the frustration of his aspirations for public service.

Tao Yuanming's Poem of Drinking Wine

Tao Yuanming (365–427), a poet and essayist of the period from the Eastern Jin to the Southern Dynasty, was born into a downfallen aristocratic family. He was a minor official for a few years, but resigned as he refused to "make curtsies for the salary of five bushels of rice." He lived in seclusion in the countryside, "picking asters beneath the eastern fence." Tao was fond of wine and was frank about his "addiction to wine" in his poems. Contemporary writers recorded his "fondness for drinking"—he used a scarf to filter wine, bought wine on credit, and passed out drunk on rocks. Once he became tipsy at a feast and said to his friends: "I'm going to sleep and you may leave." The candidness he demonstrated in an intoxicated state and his abandonment of officialdom for a rustic life in the countryside made him a great hermit. He was a role model for China's scholar-bureaucrats. Many of them followed Tao's example and chose to live in seclusion when their political aspirations were frustrated or when they became tired of bureaucracy. They sought inspiration from Tao's poetry and stories. Such people include Tang and Song Dynasty poets Bai Juyi, Su Shi, Lu You, and Xin Qiji. Tao's love affair with wine reflects the close relationship between wine and poetry creation in China's cultural history.

After taking up a rustic life, Tao wrote a suite of twenty poems on wine. The foreword of the suite reads:

"I live in seclusion without company and face long nights. Occasionally I have fine wine and spend the entire evening drinking. I drink alone until I am drunk. Once I am sober, I write a few poems to entertain myself. These poems may not have been properly composed, but my friends transcribe them, finding them amazing."

Although Tao wrote extensively about wine, only eleven of his poems refer directly to wine. Even these poems are not really odes to wine; they have other allusions and are obviously the author's expression of his emotions. Tao toiled hard in the countryside from dawn until the moon came up. From his poems, readers can appreciate the pleasure he derived from drinking wine: he sought relaxation and recreation from wine, enjoyed drinking with his friends and neighbors and took delight in talking while drinking. Unlike the "Seven Sages of the Bamboo Grove," who hid themselves completely in wine, Tao was happily resigned to his fate and his attitude towards wine was rooted in Confucian thoughts. He combined the essence of Confucian and Taoist thoughts and created a spirit that exerted a profoundly positive

Tao Yuanming Going Home Drunk, a surviving painting by the Ming period painter Zhang Peng (exact dates unknown) depicts the poet Tao Yuanming holding a chrysanthemum bloom as he drinks wine, and conveys the air of a man who has turned his back on ambition.

influence on the scholar-bureaucrats of subsequent generations. An oft-cited poem from his suite of poems on drinking wine reads:

Within the world of men I make my home,
Yet din of horse and carriage there is none;
You ask me how this quiet is achieved ——
With thoughts remote the place appears alone.
While picking asters beneath the eastern fence
My gaze upon the southern mountain rests;
The mountain views are good by day or night,
The birds come flying homeward to their nests.
A truth in this reflection lies concealed,
But I forget how it may be revealed.

In this poem, the poet indicated that although he lived in the mundane world, he stayed aloof and could avoid interference as if he were living in a remote place, even though he actually lived in a bustling town.

"Poet Immortal: Li Bai and Wine"

Li Bai is the most popular poet among the Chinese. People not only enjoy reciting his poems, but also delight in his legendary stories, the most famous being "Li Bai Getting Drunk." Once, as told by his contemporary poet Du Fu, he wrote a hundred poems after drinking a cask of wine. He was drunk in a wine shop when he received an imperial summons; he was asleep at a tavern in Chang'an when the Emperor called, but he would not board the imperial boat, saying "Your humble servant is a god of wine." This episode earned Li Bai the nickname of "god of wine." He was also a highly prolific poet, dubbed "Poet Immortal." More than 1,500 of his poems remain today. According to the historian and poet Guo Moruo (1892–1978), sixteen percent of Li's poems mention wine. Wine was indeed a source of inspiration for the poet and his greatest source of enjoyment in life.

The story "Li Bai responding to a letter from Tubo" depicts an unconventional "god of wine." The story goes that one day an envoy from Tubo presented state credentials to the Emperor of the

Tang Dynasty. The credentials were written in a tribal language that few people in the Central Plains could recognize. The envoy proclaimed that if anyone from the Tang Dynasty could read the credentials and write a reply on the spot, Tubo would pay tribute to the Tang Dynasty every year; otherwise, Tubo would no longer do so. As the people of Tubo had expected, the Tang emperor and his ministers were unable to decipher the language. At this awkward moment, someone recommended Li Bai to the emperor, so the emperor immediately summoned Li to the court to write a reply; he also ordered all civil and military officials to stand at the entrance to the imperial palace to greet Li as a gesture of respect. Yet Li was dead drunk and had to be helped into the palace. The tipsy Li scanned the Tubo credentials and told the emperor that Tubo was demanding large tracts of land from the Tang, and that if the demand was not met, they would send troops to attack the Tang. The emperor instructed him to write a reply, but Li said: "Your Majesty, I can't even stand steady. Could I ask you to rub the ink stone for me, the Queen to support my head, the Prime Minster to

A modern wine bottle with a depiction of the drunken Li Bai, produced in remembrance of the "Immortal of the Wine". (E Guoqing/China News)

take off my shoes and socks, and the eunuch to dip the brush in the ink and then place it between my toes?" The emperor had no choice but to comply. He rolled up his sleeves and started rubbing the ink stone, the Queen tenderly supported Li's head, and eunuch Gao Lishi knelt down to remove Li's shoes and socks and placed the brush between his toes. Li then lifted up his foot and composed a reply; he then read out the reply, first in Chinese and then in the Tubo language. The emperor was deeply impressed by Li's talents and granted him the title of "distinguished scholar of the Imperial Academy" on the spot. The episode spread Li's fame to Tubo.

Li Bai, who lived during a period when the Tang Dynasty was at the height of its prosperity, was heavily influenced by traditional thoughts and social mores. In his adolescence, he made up his mind to "play an instrumental role in the running of the nation" and to "resign when his missions have been accomplished." He had a strong desire to "amaze the world with a single feat" and to "soar in his career." Yet, politically, he was often marginalized and was even once exiled to the frontier.

Of his numerous great poems, *Qiang Jin Jiu*, an invitation to wine to his close friends Cen Xun and Yuan Danqiu, is generally considered the most eloquent footnote to his life and fondness for wine:

> *Do you not see the Yellow River come from the sky,*
> *Rushing into the sea and never coming back?*
> *Do you not see the mirror bright in chamber high*
> *Grieve over your snow-white hair that once was silken black?*
> *When hopes are won, oh, drink your fill in high delight*
> *And never leave your wine cup empty in moonlight!*
> *Heaven has made us talents; we're not made in vain.*
> *A thousand gold coins spent, more will turn up again.*
> *Kill a cow, cook a sheep and let us merry be,*
> *And drink three hundred cupfuls of wine in high glee!*
> *Dear friends of mine,*
> *Cheer up, cheer up!*

Qiang Jin Jiu ('*Bring in the Wine*'), a painting on a poetic theme by the contemporary artist Gu Bingxin (1923–2001).

I invite you to wine.

Do not put down your cup!

I will sing you a song, please hear,

O hear! Lend me a willing ear!

What difference will rare and costly dishes make?

I want only to get drunk and never to wake.

How many great men were forgotten through the ages?

Great drinkers are better known than sober sages.

The Prince of Poets feasted in his palace at will,

Drank wine at ten thousand coins a cask and laughed his fill.

A host should not complain of money he is short;

To drink together we'd sell things of any sort.

The fur coat worth a thousand coins of gold

And flower-dappled horse may both be sold

To buy good wine that we may drown the woes age-old.

From Wine Restaurants to Bars

The "Fan Building" in Kaifeng, Henan, where the imperial court reveled with wine, is now the most luxurious restaurant in town. (China News)

Traditional Wine Restaurants

For centuries, people have been patronizing restaurants for drinking.

In the final years of the Later Zhou Dynasty, social standards deteriorated and the ban on wine consumption was abolished. During the Eastern Zhou Dynasty, the states were at war against one another, and although wine sales were banned in the states, bootlegging persisted. It was during this period that taverns offering wine became popular. During the Warring States Period, such taverns appeared across all states, and their number and size grew steadily. According to *Records of the Grand Historian*, Jing Ke, who later attempted to assassinate the Emperor of Qin, was exceedingly fond of wine. Every day, he drank with Gao Jianli and other friends at a local tavern; when they got tipsy, Gao would play a musical instrument and Jing would sing to the music. This description suggests that in the State of Yan towards the end of the Warring States Period, taverns not only provided patrons with drinking utensils, but were also settings for entertainment.

From the Spring and Autumn and Warring States Periods to the Qin Dynasty, wine shops could be found even in remote villages. Legend has it that Liu Bang, the founding father of the Han Dynasty, was so poor in his early years that he could not afford wine and had to purchase on credit; he drank whatever wine he could find and often fell asleep when he was drunk. His unruly behavior earned him the nickname "The Rascal." Sima Xiangru, a literary giant of the Western Han Dynasty (c. 17–127 BC), ran a small wine shop with his wife Zhuo Wenjun before he made his name in the literary world. Zhuo would wear thin makeup and act as the shop clerk, while Sima would wear baggy trousers and run errands for their shop.

During the Tang Dynasty, a post-house was set up every fifteen kilometers and allowed to offer wine. These post-houses were essentially government-run taverns. In the Tang Dynasty, shops in the capital city of Chang'an were confined to two local markets, but wine shops were not restricted and could be found everywhere from busy commercial streets to back alleys. According to historic annals, the tallest wine restaurant in Chang'an soared dozens of meters high, with banners fluttering in the wind, and was visible from quite a distance.

The terms wine restaurants and teahouses appear frequently in novels written during the Song, Yuan, Ming and Qing Dynasties; they were an integral part of local markets. In Bianliang (present day Kaifeng), the capital city of the Northern Song Dynasty, there were many two or three-storied wine restaurants. The entrances to these restaurants were decorated with colored ribbons, leading to a long corridor lined by small booths, where patrons drank and made merry. The restaurants were sumptuously furnished with ornate chairs and expensive wine vessels, and the walls were adorned with paintings and calligraphic works by prominent figures. This is illustrated in *Riverside Scene at the Pure Moon Festival*, a famed painting by Zhang Zeduan of the Northern Song Dynasty.

The capital city of the Yuan Dynasty was located in what is present day Beijing. During this period, Chinese cities were expanding rapidly, and wine restaurants were set up in many large cities, such as Beijing, Hangzhou and Yangzhou. According to historic annals, the Yuan capital boasted more than one-hundred wine restaurants, each producing two to three hundred kilograms of wine per day. Back then, the capital was a boisterous city where drinking was a highly popular pastime.

In the early years of the Ming Dynasty, the first Ming emperor, Zhu Yuanzhang (1368-99), banned wine consumption, but he soon changed his mind. He even ordered the construction of wine restaurants in the capital city. When the "Drunken Immortal House" was completed, Zhu invited a large group of court officials to a banquet there. Thanks to the support of the imperial court, wine restaurants rapidly expanded in size during the Ming Dynasty, and by the end of the period, with further economic development and the expansion of commerce and industry, wine restaurants became the major structures in Chinese cities.

During the Qing Dynasty, most restaurants were also wine shops. In the later Qing Dynasty and the early years of the Republic of China, there were many sizable restaurants in Beijing's prime locations, such as Dongsi, Xidan and Gulou. They offered not only delicacies, but also fine wine. During the Republic of China period, many wine restaurants in large coastal cities such as Shanghai began to offer Western alcoholic beverages, and there were even some restaurants offering wine of homegrown brands, attracting a steady stream of patrons. Wang Baohe, one of the largest wine restaurants in Shanghai in the early twentieth century, specialized in the distribution of yellow wine from Shaoxing. The wine was characterized by strong aroma and was immensely popular among drinkers and even exported to foreign countries. These restaurants were at their busiest in autumn, when crabs matured and patrons poured in. Juicy crabs were often laid out at the restaurant entrance with price tags to entice patrons.

Bars—Leisure Venues in the Cities

Bars originated in the West, and for most Chinese people, bars are symbols of "Westernization."

The first bar in China was set up almost a century ago. The past century also saw the gradual integration of bar culture with Chinese traditional culinary culture. In the late 1920s and early 1930s, bars were very popular in Shanghai, but suffered when the Pacific War broke out. Bars did not make a comeback until the late 1980s. They first resurfaced in large cities such as Shenzhen, Guangzhou, Shanghai and Beijing and rapidly gained popularity among city dwellers.

Nanluogu Alley in Beijing is home to a thriving cluster of bars. (CFP)

In Beijing, the first bar occurred on Sanlitun Road near the district of foreign embassies. It soon expanded to become the "Sanlitun Bar District," which at its peak contained nearly 200 bars. Frequent patrons of the bars in Beijing were business people, office workers, artists, university students and foreign expatriates. Statistics show that prior to 1996, foreigners accounted for more than 95 percent of the bar clientele at Sanlitun, but that in 2003, about 70 percent of the bar clientele was Chinese. Even today, foreigners remain frequent patrons of bars at Sanlitun. Over the years, similar bar districts have also occurred at Houhai, Gulou and Luogu Alley. Bars in Beijing are generally tastefully decorated and have distinctive characteristics. A bar's style of music and decoration

The West Street in Yangshuo, Guiling, Guangxi is immensely popular among domestic and overseas tourists. This long street is lined by brick and wood buildings whose ground floors serve as souvenir shops, bars, and restaurants. Pictured here is the counter of a bar. (Aying/CFP)

At the Shangri-La Ancient Town in Yunnan, Tibetan customs and bars reflecting Western lifestyles blend perfectly. (Ru Baile/CFP)

influences its popularity among patrons. Beijing's bars come in all shapes and sizes; there is an "auto bar" based on a disused bus, a "football bar" with football related motifs, a "movie bar" where movies are screened, an "artists' bar" with a strong artistic ambience, and even a bar where the walls are adorned with vehicle number plates.

In Shanghai, bars are clustered at the Bund and on Hengshan Road, Yandang Road, Julu Road, South Maoming Road, and Duolun Road in downtown areas, where there is a large concentration of buildings of western architectural styles. Shanghai's bars are noted for their trendy and avant-garde decoration, music, topics of conversation and dress code—a reflection of the city's status as the "Oriental Capital of Fashion."

In Shenzhen, a rapidly expanding city, bars are a vital fashion statement. They are mostly of a modest size and are clustered at the Overseas Chinese City complex and Shekou Sea World; they are the favorite hangouts of the locals. The bar district at the Overseas Chinese City complex is run by young people and exudes a sense of youthfulness. The bar district at the Shekou Sea World is frequented by expatriates and has an exotic feel.

In recent years, with the growing influx of foreign visitors to China, bars have mushroomed at the popular destinations for foreign tourists, such as Lhasa, Lijiang, Dali and Guilin.

It is noteworthy that bars in China have a close relationship with the nation's pop music scene. Singers and bands are a big part of bars in large cities. Some of them perform classic Chinese and Western music, while others specialize in original music. The performers enhance the enjoyment of bar patrons and enrich the city's nightlife and they also have the opportunity to be discovered by record companies and turn professional.

At Chinese bars, the preferred drinks are beer, soda and red wine. Whisky, vodka and cocktails are also popular. In recent years, cocktail mixing at bars has become a highly fashionable job among young people, and some vocational education institutions have started courses in cocktail mixing.

For wage-earners, bars can be very expensive. The same beer which sells for less than 10 yuan in a supermarket may cost 20 to 30

Shichahai in Beijing's Xicheng District is one of the city's few open water areas, adjacent to Beijing's cultural heritage protection zone. In recent years, bars and specialty restaurants have mushroomed at Shichahai and have become favorite leisure and relaxation spots for tourists and locals alike. (Zhang Kaixin/CFP)

A bar in Beijing, featuring country music, with a nostalgic feel. (CFP)

yuan at a bar. High prices at bars have compelled many less fashion-conscious people to meet with their friends at Chinese restaurants.

Consumption of Imported Wine

In China, imported alcoholic beverages are generically referred to as "foreign wine." The importation of foreign wine through international trade dates back to the early years of the Qing Dynasty. Emperor Kangxi (1654–1722) once suffered from diarrhea and a foreign missionary cured his aliment. He advised the emperor to drink a little wine every day as a precaution against disease. The emperor heeded his advice and developed a lifelong habit of drinking wine every day; it was then that European wine was first officially introduced to China.

The Dali Ancient Town, on China's first list of major historical towns, was built in 1382, in the fifteenth year of the reign of Emperor Hong Wu of the Ming Dynasty. The town is nestled snugly between Erhai Lake to the east and Cang Mountain to the west. The Huguo Road in the town is lined by cafes, bars, eateries offering Bai ethnic snacks, and shops offering artworks made by ethnic groups. (Wu Luming/CFP)

In the late Qing Dynasty, the country was in decline and forced into a number of treaties with Eastern and Western powers, including Britain, France, Germany, Japan, Italy, and Russia. Under these treaties, China designated Guangzhou, Xiamen, Shanghai, Fuzhou, Ningbo, Tianjin, Hankou, Chongqing and Jiujiang as treaty ports. At these ports, these powers opened "foreign concessions" to protect their interests in China. Soon, Western missionaries and merchants arrived in China in large numbers, boosting the importation and consumption of a greater variety of foreign wine in China.

After the founding of the People's Republic of China in 1949, foreign wine was viewed as a Western luxury item and banned. Foreign wine did not reappear until 1978, when China opened its door to the outside world and embarked on economic reform. As

"Foreign wines" of various brands and from various places. (Maxppp/Photocome/CFP)

interaction with foreign countries increased, more Chinese people got their first taste of foreign wine and many hotels in large cities began offering foreign wine to foreign guests. In the 1980s, foreign wine was subjected to high import duties and could not be bought with Chinese currency but only with foreign exchange certificates. As a result, ordinary Chinese consumers did not get the chance to taste these special commodities.

In the 1990s, however, as the nation's economic reforms intensified, restrictions were lifted on wine sales and customers, resulting in a surge in the sales of foreign wine. In 1992, the Gello Group brought Carlo Rossi red wine to large Chinese cities such as Beijing and Shanghai and sold tens of thousands of cases a year. In early 1993, the slogan "Remy Martin brings you good luck" swept across the country in a television commercial. At that time, a 70ml Remy Martin cost about 10,000 yuan, compared with an average monthly salary of less than 1,000 yuan for Chinese workers. Expensive foreign wine was reserved for the extravagant *nouveaux riches*, and foreign wine was generally viewed as a sign of affluence and as a status symbol. Aggressive promotional campaigns for foreign wine exposed the Chinese to a form of consumerism that they had never seen before. Since then, as a fashionable commodity, foreign wine has been playing a role in shaping China's urban consumption culture.

With the constantly expanding variety of foreign wine and declining import duties, the number of shops offering foreign wine has surged, and more members of the middle class in the cities are eager to taste foreign wine. The consumption patterns of foreign wine have also changed; consumers'

Russian Vodka is made with various cereals and is popular in many cities in northern China. (imaginechina)

A bar in Nanjing hosts a French wine party to attract customers. (CFP)

preference has shifted from expensive wine to wine from certain places, and they have become more sophisticated in purchasing foreign wine. Foreign wine has made a considerable impact on traditional Chinese lifestyles and consumption patterns, and it has exposed Chinese consumers to the wine culture of the Western world.

Appendix:
Chronological Table of the Chinese Dynasties

The Paleolithic Period	c. 1,700,000–10,000 years ago
The Neolithic Period	c. 10,000–4,000 years ago
Xia Dynasty	2070–1600 BC
Shang Dynasty	1600–1046 BC
Western Zhou Dynasty	1046–771 BC
Spring and Autumn Period	770–476 BC
Warring States Period	475–221 BC
Qin Dynasty	221–206 BC
Western Han Dynasty	206 BC–AD 25
Eastern Han Dynasty	25–220
Three Kingdoms	220–280
Western Jin Dynasty	265–317
Eastern Jin Dynasty	317–420
Northern and Southern Dynasties	420–589
Sui Dynasty	581–618
Tang Dynasty	618–907
Five Dynasties	907–960
Northern Song Dynasty	960–1127
Southern Song Dynasty	1127–1276
Yuan Dynasty	1276–1368
Ming Dynasty	1368–1644
Qing Dynasty	1644–1911
Republic of China	1912–1949
People's Republic of China	Founded in 1949